ENTERPRISE WITHOUT
UNIONS

MANAGING WORK AND ORGANIZATIONS SERIES

Edited by Graeme Salaman, Senior Lecturer in the Faculty of Social Sciences and the Open Business School, the Open University

Current and forthcoming titles include:

Peter Anthony: *Managing Culture*
Michael Armstrong: *Managing Reward Systems*
David Casey: *Managing Learning in Organizations*
Rohan Collier: *Combatting Sexual Harassment in the Workplace*
Patricia Findlay: *Managing Company Employment Policy*
Paul Iles: *Managing Assessment Processes*
Ian McLoughlin and Stephen Gourlay: *Enterprise Without Unions*
Graeme Salaman: *Managing*
John Storey and Keith Sisson: *Managing Human Resources and Industrial Relations*

ENTERPRISE WITHOUT UNIONS
INDUSTRIAL RELATIONS IN THE NON-UNION FIRM

Ian McLoughlin and
Stephen Gourlay

Open University Press
Buckingham · Philadelphia

658.
315
MAC

Open University Press
Celtic Court
22 Ballmoor
Buckingham
MK18 1XW

and

1900 Frost Road, Suite 101
Bristol, PA 19007, USA

First Published 1994

A catalogue record of this book is available from the British Library

ISBN   0 335 19030 8 (pb)   0 335 19031 6 (hb)

A Library of Congress Cataloging-in-Publication Number is available
for this book

Typeset by Type Study, Scarborough
Printed in Great Britain by St Edmundsbury Press Ltd,
Bury St Edmunds, Suffolk

23-8-95.
D

CONTENTS

LIST OF TABLES AND FIGURES

Tables

Figures

PREFACE AND ACKNOWLEDGEMENTS

The research upon which this book is based began life in the mid–1980s as a series of discussions between Ian McLoughlin and Ian Beardwell. Under the watchful eye of a Sergeant Bilko poster, the outlines of a project which investigated the increasingly topical but largely unresearched phenomenon of industrial relations in the non-union firm took shape. Initial pump-priming funding was obtained from the Kingston Business School, and subsequently the National Advisory Board. Further funding for exploratory work was obtained from the Economic and Social Research Council's (ESRC) New Technology and the Firm Initiative (F2420026). Finally, a major award was received from the ESRC which enabled the employment of Stephen Gourlay as a research fellow (R000231164). Naturally, we would like to acknowledge the support of the funding bodies, and also thank Kingston Business School and Brunel University who hosted the research.

As with all large research projects, a complex division of labour evolved and numerous individuals became involved in one way or another during the project's life cycle. The detailed design of the project, and most of the fieldwork and qualitative data analysis were conducted by Ian McLoughlin and Stephen Gourlay. Stephen also undertook the statistical analysis for the postal

and employee surveys and assisted in the editing of the manu-
script for this volume. Ian Beardwell contributed at various
points. Along the way, Sue Bandy, John Kitching, Paul Killen
and Martin Mansfield made valued contributions as research
assistants, while numerous administrative staff and students
helped us with the seemingly endless task of transcribing
interview tapes. Thanks are due to all of these individuals. We
would also like to thank Adrian Woods for his help in the latter
stage of the project in unravelling some of the mysteries of SPSS,
and John Skelton of the Open University Press and the editor of
this series for their part in the book's production.

Ultimately, of course, the success of the project was dependent
upon the participation of a large number of firms, their managers
and their employees. We would like to thank all of them for their
assistance and forbearance. Particular thanks should go to Eddie
Cappleman, Ray Maskell and Alan Benfell, who were our main
contacts and 'champions' within the case-study firms.

Finally, the text for this volume was written by Ian McLoughlin. He would like to thank Sue (and Ellen!) for her patience in
coping with a partner who often appeared to be listening while
really in deep thought about something completely different!

Ian McLoughlin
Hampton

ABBREVIATIONS

ACAS	Advisory, Conciliation and Arbitration Service
AEEU	Amalgamated Engineering and Electrical Union (formerly AEU and AUEW)
AEU	Amalgamated Engineering Union (now part of AEEU)
ASTMS	Association of Scientific, Technical and Managerial Staffs (now part of MSF)
AUEW	Amalgamated Union of Engineering Workers (now part of AEEU)
CAD	Computer Aided Design
DTI	Department of Trade and Industry
EETPU	Electrical, Electronic and Telecommunications and Plumbing Union (now part of AEEU)
ESRC	Economic and Social Research Council
GCHQ	Government Communications Headquarters
HRM	Human Resource Management
IBM	International Business Machines
IPCS	Institution of Professional Civil Servants
MSF	Manufacturing, Science and Finance Union
TGWU	Transport and General Workers' Union
WIRS	Workplace Industrial Relations Survey

INTRODUCTION

At midday on 2 March 1989 Gareth Morris walked out of the gates of GCHQ, the government's electronic intelligence gathering centre in Cheltenham, for the last time.[1] Mr Morris had been sacked, ending 40 years of trade union membership at GCHQ. He was the last union member left at the centre, a ban on the membership of independent trade unions having been instituted some five years earlier by Mrs Thatcher's Conservative government, 'in the interests of national security'. Mr Morris was one of 14 'refuseniks' who, as a matter of principle, had turned down the £1000 inducement offered to give up their membership of the IPCS. Despite a one-day strike with other civil service unions, legal action against the government and an appeal to the International Labour Organization, the government's ban against independent trade union organization was upheld.

A recent text on contemporary industrial relations referred to the events at GCHQ as a '*cause célèbre* of the 1980s' and 'perhaps symbolic of the Government's basic attitude to trade unions' (Kessler and Bayliss, 1992: 114–15). This attitude was one which held that trade unions were a barrier to the efficient operation of the labour market and that employers should look to non-union firms for examples of how to manage their industrial relations. This meant non-union employers refusing union recognition and unionized employers resisting the extension of unionization to new locations while trying to limit union influence at existing establishments. Ideally, unions should be derecognized. 'The banning of trade unions at GCHQ . . . showed that the government was prepared to practice what it preached' (Kessler and Bayliss, 1992: 61).

Government policy and practice since 1979 has also been instrumental in placing non-unionism and the non-union enterprise firmly on the industrial relations agenda in a variety of other more pervasive ways. For example, a succession of new labour laws restricting trade unions has been passed, while policy statements have frequently espoused a view that trade unions and collective bargaining are an increasingly redundant feature in a 'modern' economy (see, for example, Department of Trade and Industry, 1990; Department of Employment, 1991; 1992). Combined with the effects of two major recessions, several major union defeats in set-piece industrial disputes, and the supposed widespread adoption of new management techniques of 'human resource management' (HRM), these views have given credence to an assumption that a major transformation in UK industrial relations has taken place. Indeed, one commentator has gone as far as to claim that non-unionism is 'now dominant in Britain' (Bassett, 1988), while a host of others, writing from a variety of perspectives, have questioned the long-term survival of collective industrial relations (see, for example, Roberts, 1987; Hanson, 1991; MacInnes, 1990; Smith and Morton, 1993).

Having said this, the weight of academic industrial relations opinion has tended to stress continuity rather than change, and at most talk of 'transition' rather than 'transformation' (Batstone and Gourlay, 1986; Millward and Stevens, 1986; Batstone, 1988; MacInnes, 1988; 1990; Evans, 1989; Marchington and Parker, 1990; Kessler and Bayliss, 1992). As a result, perhaps, non-unionism and the non-union firm have been a peculiarly neglected area of contemporary research and study. Indeed, non-unionism has never figured as a particularly important topic for industrial relations researchers. In the past, non-union industrial relations have tended to be regarded as aberrant or anachronistic in the context of a rising level of unionization and the extension of collective bargaining, or as a specific phenomenon associated

2

with 'small businesses'. In 1980, for example, an article in *Management Today* declared non-union firms to be 'outmoded relics' and a 'vanishing species' (Newman, 1980). As one commentator has recently observed, 'a very full and important agenda still awaits the attention of industrial relations researchers in this particular area' (Beaumont, 1990: 20).

Our objective is to begin to rectify this 'blind spot' in industrial relations research. One consequence of a lack of hard evidence has been that a number of largely unsubstantiated images of non-union industrial relations have been able to gain ground in recent years. For example, not only has non-unionism been declared the 'dominant' form of industrial relations, but also non-union firms are portrayed as the locus of current 'best practice' in the management of employees. Similarly, the non-union employee has been characterized as prototypical of the 'new worker' for whom individual rather than collective values are paramount, while the non-union settings which they populate are assumed to be inherently receptive to technical and other innovations and, as a result, to be highly productive.

In this book we aim to test this largely favourable and benign image of non-unionism and the non-union firm against the reality of industrial relations where unions are absent. In particular we will address the following key questions:

- What has been the nature and extent of the decline of collective industrial relations – how 'dominant' is non-unionism?
- What in conceptual terms are the issues raised by the absence of unions for the management of the employment relationship, and what is 'new' and 'distinctive' about 'human resource management'?
- How in practice do non-union firms manage personnel and industrial relations matters[2] and to what extent are new HRM techniques actually involved?
- Why do employees in non-union settings not join unions?
- And to what extent are managers really better able to implement significant technical and related organizational change, in the absence of unions?

In addressing these questions we have chosen to concentrate on the phenomenon of non-unionism and the non-union firm as they manifest themselves in what can broadly be defined as the 'high-technology' sector of the economy. The main reason being that the sector is often associated with many of the exemplars of the non-union approach and accordingly as being one where 'leading-edge' HRM practices are highly prevalent (see, for example, Bassett, 1986). However, this perception is mostly based on journalistic and practitioner accounts of 'best practice' in household-name firms such as IBM (Peach, 1983).

The purpose of the research study upon which this book is based was to subject industrial relations in non-union settings to a more rigorous scrutiny. The research design incorporated a combination of survey and in-depth case-study methods and the data set upon which we will draw comprises:

- a postal questionnaire survey of the extent of non-unionism, and the link between this and technical and organizational change, in 115 establishments with over 100 employees;
- a follow-up interview survey with personnel specialists, or the senior manager responsible for personnel matters, to explore management policies and practices at 30 of these locations;
- detailed case studies conducted over several months of management policies and practices in three non-union firms – a computer company, a consumer electronics firm and a contract design company – involving interviews with management respondents from managing director to first line level;
- attitude surveys of a sample of the core workforce at each of these case-study firms, the employee samples ranging from manual shop-floor operatives, through white-collar office workers, to engineering technicians and computer professionals.

The research took place in establishments and firms located in the South East of England. This is an area noted for historically lower levels of union organization and influence and, more recently, for the spatial clustering of growing high-technology industries, especially in and around towns along the M4/M3/M27 corridor (Beaumont and Harris, 1988; Millward and Stevens, 1988; Morgan and Sayer, 1988; Causer and Jones, 1992). Fieldwork was conducted between 1988 and 1991 and further details of the research methodology are given in the Appendix.

4

The book is structured into seven chapters as follows. In Chapter 1 we explore the context of the rise of the non-union firm by examining the nature and extent of the decline of collective industrial relations in Britain since 1979. In Chapter 2, existing theoretical and conceptual approaches to the role of management style in industrial relations are discussed with a view to providing a conceptual framework within which we can locate approaches, such as HRM, in non-union settings. Chapters 3–6 are devoted to a discussion of our research findings. Chapter 3 examines the extent of non-unionism and the nature of management style in the high-technology sector. Chapter 4 provides a more detailed examination of the management of industrial relations in our three case-study enterprises. Chapter 5 is concerned with why individual employees in these three firms did not join unions. Chapter 6 explores how change, in particular technical and related organizational change, was managed in the absence of unions. Finally, Chapter 7 draws together the threads of the analysis, and asks if a non-union system of industrial relations will become dominant in Britain in the 1990s. In answer to this question we sketch three possible scenarios. While each has different implications, none points to a decline in the significance of non-unionism and the non-union firm in the foreseeable future.

Note

1 For an account of the banning of unions at GCHQ see Lanning and Norton-Taylor (1991).
2 For the sake of brevity we sometimes use the term personnel to refer to both personnel and industrial relations matters in the text, especially when discussing our own research findings.

THE DECLINE OF COLLECTIVE INDUSTRIAL RELATIONS

Introduction

The purpose of this chapter is to assess the decline of collective industrial relations in Britain. As already suggested, for some non-unionism is now a dominant feature while for others the extent and significance of decline is largely overstated. It is this debate which provides the context for our interest in non-unionism and the non-union firm. A key stimulus here has been a similar debate in the USA, where it has been claimed a non-union system of industrial relations has now become established. For some this is seen as being indicative of current and likely future trends in Britain. We begin this chapter, therefore, by considering the decline of trade unions and the rise of non-unionism in the USA. We then turn directly to a consideration of contemporary developments in British industrial relations.

The decline of trade union organization in the USA: a model for Britain?

In part, attention has been drawn to the issue of non-unionism in Britain by experience in the USA. In 1992, after a prolonged period of decline which began in the mid–1950s, just over 11 per cent of the private sector workforce was organized by trade unions (Meyer and Cooke, 1993). As a consequence, there has been a considerable debate regarding the 'transformation' of the industrial relations system and the emergence of non-unionism and the non-union firm as dominant features of it (see, for example, *Business Week*, 1981; Edwards and Podgursky, 1986; Kochan *et al.*, 1986; Hoerr, 1991). According to Kochan *et al.* (1986: 79), the decline in union organization in the USA has been 'a function of a changing environment, deep-seated managerial values opposed to unions, and increased opportunities and incentives to avoid unions resulting from changing competitive and cost conditions'. In particular, increased global competition, the changing characteristics of product markets (for example, changes in consumer tastes and deregulation) and the adoption of new technologies and production techniques have combined to present organizations with new problems and opportunities. One effect has been to allow an 'unfreezing' of existing employment relationships, by providing firms with an opportunity to review their current practices and restructure to suit new circumstances (Kochan and Tamir, 1989).

One of the key 'strategic choices' that US managers have confronted in this respect has been in relation to trade union organization and collective bargaining. Kochan and his colleagues argue that the deep-seated ideological opposition to trade unions embedded in the values of American management and the culture of many American organizations has led in many instances to a complete rejection of trade unions. In others it has led to an attempt to restrict union influence, either, by decentralizing collective bargaining and limiting recognition to manual and routine white-collar employees or, by forging new co-operative bargaining relationships, often on the back of major concessions by the trade unions themselves, but with promised long-term benefits of greater job security and employee involvement. A key factor has been the development and diffusion of new 'human resource management' techniques by 'leading-edge' firms in new and growing sectors such as high technology. These have provided an alternative model for managing without trade unions. Indeed, the effectiveness of HRM has, it is claimed, given non-union firms a competitive advantage over their unionized counterparts, rendering the former 'essentially immune' from unionization and providing the latter with a strong incentive to deunionize (Kochan *et al.*, 1986: 54–5).

What are the implications of developments in the USA for British industrial relations? For some commentators the simple message to be drawn is that past US experience indicates the future trend for Britain (see, for example, Lloyd, 1987). For others, the experience and context of trade unionism in the USA are virtually unique and hence of little or no use as a guide to potential developments in the British context (Kelly, 1988). Both views, in particular the first, are probably too simplistic.

For example, one objection to the application of the Kochan *et al.* thesis to Britain is that British employers and managers simply do not harbour the deep-seated opposition to trade unions of their US counterparts and have no desire to terminate existing bargaining relationships, or to resist the initiation of new ones. However, Beaumont (1987: 32–4) argues that the American experience cannot be disregarded on such grounds. Historical evidence reveals considerable variations in British employer attitudes and responses to trade unions within and between industries. Moreover, white-collar unionization has only been accepted by British employers under pressure from government at the key junctures provided by the two world wars. A more plausible argument is that unionization in Britain has historically attained far higher levels than ever experienced in America. This has created traditions and expectations of union organization beyond those ever achieved in the USA. Thus, the question hinges not so much on British employers' desire to deunionize as on their *capacity* to do so.

For example, one means by which American employers can become non-union or resist unionization is the legal mechanism of the certification/decertification election. This provides for the ratification of union representation through employee ballots and gives American employers a clear focus and a variety of opportunities for resisting unionization before, during and even after a certification election. However, in the main, such legal devices have not been available in Britain.[1] In this and other ways, argues Beaumont, British employers have, in the past at least, been far more constrained than their US counterparts in the means at their disposal to become non-union (Beaumont, 1987: 33). However, changes made since 1979 by successive Conservative governments to the legal framework of industrial relations in Britain have, in many eyes, been designed to increase the capacity of both employers and employees to choose to conduct their affairs without unions. Given this, at least one commentator has suggested that Britain 'is the most likely country in Europe' where the growth of a non-union system could occur (Beaumont, 1987: 51, citing Barbash, 1984). To what extent, then, has there been a decline in collective industrial relations, and is non-unionism now dominant in Britain?

The decline of collective industrial relations in Britain

It is widely recognized that 'the 1980s was a decade of profound economic, political and social change' (Kessler and Bayliss, 1992: 235). For example, changes occurred in the political environment, with a fundamental shift towards free-market economics and a rejection of Keynsian economics and 'corporatism' (MacInnes, 1988). In economic terms the period was one which started and ended with recession and high unemployment and in which product markets became increasingly competitive (Kelly, 1990; Marchington and Parker, 1990). Finally, there were continuing changes in the social environment and class structure, in particular an extension of 'privatized' and 'individualist' attitudes and values, which some claim has been at the expense of 'collectivism' among increasing numbers of working people (see, for example, Phelps-Brown, 1990).

While all of the above political, economic and social changes had implications for industrial relations, it is the changes in government labour-market policy and the legal framework that most observers have seen as of greatest significance. The policies that have been pursued by successive Conservative governments since 1979 have been based on the premise that trades unions 'are a hindrance to the proper working of the labour market' (Kessler and Bayliss, 1992: 236). This has been reflected in a succession of legal reforms which have sought to break 'trade union monopoly power' (McIlroy, 1991). These have variously sought to: cease the statutory supports and political encouragement for the extension of collective bargaining (Beaumont, 1987); free employees from institutionalized constraints which 'force' them to remain union members for reasons other than positive choice (Dunn, 1989); depoliticize trade unions by weakening links with the Labour Party by requiring compulsory ballots on the political levy and outlawing 'political' and 'solidarity' strikes (Evans, 1990); reduce the significance of collective decision-making in unions through statutory requirements for balloting of individual union members in union elections and before industrial action (Martin *et al.*, 1991); restrict the scope of trade unions to organize and engage in industrial action (Metcalfe and Dunn, 1989); and abandon labour inclusion in state policy-making (Crouch, 1989).

However, the extent to which a decline in collective industrial relations, has been a direct result of these changes, is far from clear-cut. For example, the impact of legal reforms on the conduct of industrial relations has been contradictory and ambiguous (Evans, 1985; 1987; ACAS, 1989; Metcalfe and Dunn, 1989; Kelly, 1990; Martin *et al.*, 1991; Incomes Data Services, 1992). Some have argued that, in reality, the capacity given to employers and individual employees to exercise choice in relation to trade unions, and the manner in which the unions themselves are circumscribed, has not been that dramatic. Others have observed that employers (and for that matter employees) have appeared reluctant to act on their new-found capacities. Moreover, despite the intention behind them, legal changes such as compulsory ballots over industrial action or political funds have often appeared to act to the advantage of trade unions, by providing an irrefutable mandate in their favour.

Given this, some right-wing analysts of the Conservative record still perceive the need for further legal changes if British industrial relations are to be adequately 'decollectivized' (see, for example, Hanson, 1991). In any event, in the wake of the perceived failings of previous reforms, new legislation has subsequently been enacted or proposed, abolishing the provisions on closed-shop ballots, seeking to restrict strikes in essential services, revising the existing arrangements governing union 'check-off' agreements, and making it lawful for employers to offer superior pay and conditions to employees who have agreed to accept a personal contract rather than be subject to collective agreements (Smith and Morton, 1994).

If, at the level of policy and legal frameworks, the extent to which decollectivization has occurred is unclear, how far is this borne out at workplace level? In order to explore this question we will focus on four key areas: trade union membership and density; union recognition and derecognition; the coverage and structure of collective bargaining; and the performance of non-union firms relative to their unionized counterparts.

The decline of trade union membership and density?

The most obvious test of any decline in collective industrial relations is a marked fall in the aggregate number and proportion of potential members who are organized by trade unions (trade union density). That aggregate union membership and density have fallen in Britain since 1979 is not disputed. However, there is far from a consensus about the extent, significance and explanation of this decline (for various views, see Bain and Price, 1983; Disney, 1990; Freeman and Pelletier, 1990; Runciman, 1991; Waddington, 1992). Part of the difficulty here is the many ways in which union density can be calculated and problems with the accuracy of the union membership figures that are used (Kelly and Bailey, 1989: 54–5).

If we take 'employment density'[2] as the main indicator of the extent of union organization, then, according to Department of Employment statistics, a decline of 12.7 percentage points to just over 44.2 per cent has taken place since 1979 (Kessler and Bayliss, 1992: 136–42).[3] This represents a loss of 3 million union members for TUC and non-TUC unions, effectively wiping out the membership gains of the 1970s. Moreover, since 1984, as employment has expanded the rate of decline in employment density has increased. This is most worrying for unions since it means they have been unable to recruit sufficient members in expanding areas to compensate for continued losses in contracting areas. In the private sector, especially, unionism has remained entrenched

11

Table 1.1 Key changes in workplace industrial relations, 1980–90 (per cent)

	1980	1984	1990
No union members among:			
Manual employees	36	32	42
Non-manual employees	45	42	49
All employees	27	27	36
No recognized unions present:			
Private manufacturing	35	44	56
Private services	59	56	64
All (including public sector)	36	34	47
No recognized manual unions:			
Private manufacturing	35	45	56
Private services	67	62	69
All (including public sector)	45	38	52
Proportion of employees covered by collective bargaining:			
Private sector	*	52	44
All (including public sector)	*	71	54

* Information on the coverage of collective bargaining was not collected by the 1980 survey.
Sources: Millward and Stevens (1986); Millward *et al.* (1992)

in industries with high levels of union density but has failed to grow in poorly organized industries which expanded in number as employment within them grew (see Kelly, 1990: 67–9; Waddington, 1992: 289–302).

One manifestation of this trend at workplace level would be an increase in the proportion of workplaces with no union members present (that is, zero union density). According to the Workplace Industrial Relations Survey (WIRS) series, a sizeable increase in the proportion of private sector workplaces with no trade union members present did take place in the 1980s (see Table 1.1). In the first years of the decade this increase was largely explained by recession. This resulted in the disproportionate closure and loss of employment in large unionized establishments, especially in private manufacturing (Millward and Stevens, 1986:60). However, in the second half of the 1980s there appeared to have 'been a substantial drift away from union membership' on the part of individual employees, which could not be explained entirely as a result of a loss of employment (Millward et al., 1992:67, 352; see also Gregg and Yates, 1991:365). This could be taken to suggest that individuals still in employment were now resigning from trade union membership or simply choosing not to join in the first place, possibly because of more individualistic attitudes and/or the legal removal of institutional constraints which hitherto forced them to join.

A growth of union derecognition?

A further key test of the decline of collective industrial relations is the extent to which employers have withdrawn support for trade union recognition. One indicator of this would be a rise in the proportion of establishments without recognized unions due to employers in existing establishments engaging in derecognition.

According to the 1990 WIRS, the proportion of all private and public sector workplaces with no recognized trade unions present increased from 34 per cent in 1984 to 47 per cent in 1990 (see Table 1.1). In private manufacturing this trend was evident throughout the 1980s, with an increase from 35 per cent in 1980 to 56 per cent in 1990. Having said this, the increase in establishments without recognized unions in the early 1980s was explained not by derecognition but rather, once again, by the disproportionate closure of large unionized manufacturing plants due to recession (Millward and Stevens; 1986:64–9). However, the 1990 survey suggested derecognition had become more widespread in the latter part of the decade and was on the increase (a view supported by other smaller-scale surveys; see, for example, Edwards and Marginson, 1988; ACAS, 1989; Claydon, 1989; Smith and Morton, 1990; Gregg and Yates 1991). Most notably, nearly one-fifth of the WIRS panel survey

13

establishments which recognized unions in 1984 did not have any in 1990, while only one-tenth of establishments without recognized unions in 1984 had recognized unions in 1990 (Millward *et al.*, 1992: 75).

Alongside the decline in recognition must also be set the reluctance of both existing non-union establishments and newly formed establishments to grant recognition. The WIRS 1990 survey noted that the proportion of existing establishments that had granted new recognition in the three years before the survey was less than 1 per cent of all private sector establishments (Millward *et al.*, 1992: 74–5). The survey also suggested that new establishments were much less likely to recognize unions than older establishments. For example, private sector workplaces that were less than ten years old recognized unions in just over one-fifth of cases, compared to just over half of those that were more than 20 years old. Interestingly, the relationship between age and recognition was not smooth, with the youngest the least likely to recognize and the oldest the most. Rather, establishments which were between seven and ten years old – that is, founded in the early 1980s – had the lowest level of recognition (Millward *et al.*, 1992: 73).

A retreat from collective bargaining?

A further significant area in which a decline in collective industrial relations might be expected to be manifested is in the coverage and structure of collective bargaining. The first and most obvious indicator of such a trend would be a reduction in the proportion of employees who have their terms and conditions determined by this means. The WIRS series records a fall in aggregate coverage from 71 per cent in 1984 to 54 per cent in 1990 (see Table 1.1). In the private sector coverage dropped from 52 per cent to 41 per cent. Thus by 1990 a minority of employees in the private sector had their pay and conditions determined by collective bargaining. The authors of the survey note that this trend represented 'one of the most dramatic changes in the character of British industrial relations that our survey has measured' (Millward *et al.*, 1992: 93).

Changes in the level of collective bargaining, in particular a move towards decentralization from multi-employer to single-employer, and from single-employer to multi-plant, may also be an important indicator. In the USA, centralized bargaining structures have been identified as a significant constraint on the process of deunionization in industries and firms where they are present (Kochan *et al.*, 1986: 60–2).[4] More generally, cross-national studies show unionisation levels appear to have held up least well in countries with more decentralized bargaining structures (Freeman, 1988).

In Britain some observers see decentralization as the 'dominant de-collectivist policy' (Smith and Morton, 1990: 6). It has been argued that the decentralization of bargaining from the company to the plant level results in an 'institutional separation' of plant-based bargaining from strategic decision-makers who retain control at arms' length (Marchington and Parker, 1990: 29–32). According to Smith and Morton (1990: 7), such 'institutional separation' has been designed to confine union activity to the level of the 'business unit' and fits neatly with legal constrictions intended similarly to confine industrial action. Similarly, Beaumont (1990: 267) suggests that decentralization from the national or multi-employer level makes recognition decisions and the role of collective bargaining more '*individual*-employer specific' (emphasis in original).

While the evidence of a decline in multi-employer bargaining in much of the private sector has been apparent since the 1970s (Daniel and Millward, 1983; Millward and Stevens, 1986; Gregg and Yates, 1991; Millward *et al.*, 1992; Brown, 1993), the extent to which a trend towards decentralization from company-level to plant-level bargaining has taken place since 1979 is far from clear-cut. For example, decentralization has not usually extended all the way down to establishment level, but rather involved only a withdrawal from industry-wide arrangements (Brown and Walsh, 1991). At the same time, a greater proportion of employers in the private sector, particularly in private services, have chosen to move in the opposite direction and have adopted more centralized arrangements at company level, having previously bargained mainly at plant level (Beaumont, 1990: 117–18: Millward *et al.*, 1992). This is confirmed by the WIRS surveys. According to the authors of the 1990 survey, 'rather than lead to more plant-level negotiations, the move away from multi-employer negotiations was accompanied by an increase in negotiating structures at enterprise or company level' (Millward *et al.*, 1992: 255).

Moreover, whatever the actual trends towards decentraliz-ation, the extent to which it can be interpreted unambiguously as an index of employer strategies to decollectivize their employ-ment relations, possibly as a precursor to derecognition, is open to considerable doubt. For example, Jackson *et al.* (1991–2) note that the motivations for decentralization on the part of employers are mixed and that there is no single explanation applicable to all cases. Similarly, Marchington and Parker (1990: 213) point out that 'institutional separation' cannot be assumed to be done principally in order to marginalize trade unions. Labour relations may only be a secondary consideration in such decisions.

Aside from reducing the number of employees who are covered and changing the level at which it takes place, a move towards deunionization might also be seen as indicated by a change in the scope of collective bargaining, in terms both of a reduction in the range of issues over which negotiation occurs, and of the number of employees, or bargaining units, that are covered. In fact, the WIRS series shows quite clearly that the range of issues over which collective bargaining occurs has become narrower since 1980, especially in the early part of the decade, and in the context of the overall decline of collective bargaining (Millward *et al.*, 1992: 352–3). The complexity of union representation in terms of numbers of recognized trade unions and bargaining units, on the other hand, has shown much less change than has taken place in terms of recognition and bargaining coverage (Millward *et al.*, 1992: 102).

While such institutional arrangements may not have changed substantially, Kessler and Bayliss (1992) suggest that the use to which they are put, has. This is because managements are now more able to use their advantageous labour-market position to push through substantive changes in the employment relation-ship, for example by 'something for something' bargaining where pay increases are tied explicitly to changes in working practices (Kessler and Bayliss, 1992: 182). In some cases this advantage has gone as far as the securing of new procedure agreements which enshrine managerial prerogative over matters such as the movement and flexibility of labour (Kessler and Bayliss, 1992: 182). This has been most notable on 'greenfield' sites where unions have only been able to secure recognition by offering major concessions in the form of 'new-style' single-union agreements. For critics, some of these agreements amount to little more than 'legitimized non-unionism' (Rico, 1987; TUC, 1988).

However, the extent to which these changes can be seen unambiguously as deliberate steps on the way to complete deunionization is also highly problematic. Arguably, attempts to simplify bargaining arrangements, for example the introduction of single-table bargaining, can strengthen the union position within the enterprise rather than weaken it (TUC, 1989). In addition, the shift in the 'frontier of control' towards management, in terms of both the range of issues and the outcomes of negotiations, can be viewed as a cyclical phenomenon which will eventually return the bargaining advantage to the trade unions (Batstone, 1989; Kelly, 1990). Moreover, while there have been reports that single-union agreements have resulted in few actual union members, it is also the case that companies with such arrangements have a vested interest in encouraging union membership if the credibility of the agreement is not to be compromised (Wickens, 1987). In any case, despite the visibility of 'new-style' agreements, they are few in number and their significance as a generalizable model of workplace industrial relations should not be overstated (MacInnes, 1990: 210).

A non-union incentive?

Much of the debate regarding changes in the British system of industrial relations has focused upon the question of institutional change. However, it has also been suggested that there is a need to examine industrial relations outcomes such as wage levels, productivity, investment in new technology and the general economic performance of the establishment or firm (Metcalfe, 1989). Of particular importance here is the question of whether non-union settings perform better in terms of such outcomes than their unionized counterparts. If so, then there may be a clear-cut economic incentive, as Kochan *et al.* argue exists in the USA, for unionized firms to consider deunionization and for non-union ones to continue to resist union organization.

One area in which it is often implied that non-union firms have an advantage over their unionized counterparts in Britain has been in relation to technical change (Department of Employment, 1981; Barnett, 1986). In fact, a rapid diffusion of new technologies has been a major feature of change at workplace level in Britain during the 1980s (Daniel, 1987; Daniel and Millward, 1993). For some, the increased capacity of management to undertake such widespread innovation and related organizational change is attributed to the parallel decline in trade unions which, they argue, have acted in the past as a barrier to change (see McLoughlin and Clark, 1994, for discussion).

The notion of trade unions as a barrier to change focuses on what Freeman and Medoff (1984) term the 'monopoly effect' associated with union presence. For example, by bargaining higher pay increases (the union mark-up) and enforcing union claims through restrictive practices, industrial action and so on, trade unions can resist or effectively veto changes in technology and related changes in the organization of production which might improve the productivity and performance of the firm (McLoughlin, 1993). However, Freeman and Medoff also identified a second effect associated with union presence which may have beneficial consequences when technical and related organizational change are attempted. Unions, they suggest, also provide a channel of communication and means of conflict resolution enabling co-operation with management over technical change and work organization, encouraging more effective implementation and operation of new technologies and working methods. Production is thereby more efficient, sources of conflict and grievance reduced, and the incidence of workers utilizing performance-damaging 'exit options' (absenteeism, quitting and so on), cut. This is termed the 'collective voice' effect associated with union presence and acts to enhance productivity and the performance of the firm.

Given these potential union influences, it is highly significant that available evidence from the WIRS series suggests that, when it comes to technical change in Britain, unionized workplaces may have enjoyed an advantage over their non-union counterparts. First, establishments which recognized trade unions are more, not less, likely to have introduced advanced technical change than their non-union counterparts (Daniel, 1987: 34–6, 47; Daniel and Millward, 1993; see also Latrielle, 1992). Second, there is also evidence that managements in non-union settings are less likely to consult employees over technical change than those in unionized workplaces. This is important because such consultation is associated with the successful introduction of technical change (see Daniel, 1987: 119–21, 137–8; Daniel and Millward, 1993). These findings might be taken to suggest that non-union firms not only have failed to capitalize on any advantage associated with the absence of monopoly effects, but also, and more important, have not been willing or able to find an effective substitute for the absence of the collective voice effects associated with union presence.

It is also worth noting findings concerning the influence of union presence on productivity outcomes, which might in part be related to the success of the introduction of technical and related organizational change. For example, Metcalfe (1989) argues that the weakening of the trade union 'monopoly effect' is an important element of the explanation of productivity improvement since 1979 (for a criticism of this view, see Nolan and Marginson, 1990). When it comes to the relative performance of unionized and non-union firms, Metcalfe (1990: 3) cautiously concludes that 'the net (output-weighted) association between unions and labour productivity is clearly negative' (see also Ingram and Lindop, 1990: 35).

However, a number of qualifications are made (Metcalfe, 1990: 11–12) which weaken this conclusion, if it is taken to mean that trade union presence is automatically bad for productivity and, by implication, that non-unionism is good. For example, as Metcalfe puts it, 'it takes two to tango'. That is, the effect of unions on productivity is a function of the quality of their interaction with management. This implies that the effect of union absence on productivity, and for that matter technical change, is also related to the quality of management's approach. The extent to which there is a non-union incentive, therefore, appears to be bound up with what managers actually do when it comes to managing employees in non-union settings, not just the absence of trade unions – for example, how they cope with finding an alternative to the collective voice effect associated with union presence. This brings us neatly to the subject of the next chapter which is concerned with management style in non-union firms.

Conclusion

Has there been a decline in collective industrial relations in Britain, and is non-unionism now dominant? The answer to the first part of this question is clearly yes, although identifying the extent and the factors which might explain it means that the answer to the second part must be more qualified. As far as changes in the legal framework are concerned, for example, employers in Britain have enjoyed a significant increase in their capacity to marginalize, or even choose to manage without, unions. In addition, product-market and other environmental pressures, which might have been expected to trigger a review of industrial relations practices, have also increased. At the same time, much does appear to have changed in relation to union membership and density, union recognition, and the coverage and structure of collective bargaining.

However, the extent to which these changes are wholly, or even mainly, explained by a general rejection of trade unions and collective bargaining on the part of employers, managers and employees is far from convincing. The effect of the law on the conduct of industrial relations is far from clear-cut, while recession, plant closure and redundancy appear to explain much of the decline in union membership and the fall in the extent of union recognition. Similarly, while there has been a significant decline in the coverage of collective bargaining, underlying changes in bargaining structure do not point unambiguously towards an employer strategy of decollectivization. Finally, a 'non-union incentive' does not appear to have been established. Indeed, when it comes to technical change unionized firms may well be better off. Thus, although non-unionism, especially in the private sector, is numerically dominant (or nearly so) on key dimensions such as union density, recognition and so on, the factors which explain this do not necessarily point to fundamental attitudinal and behavioural changes on the part of managers and employees themselves. If there has been a decline in collective – or more accurately, as we shall suggest in the next chapter, trade-union-based industrial relations – this has not been directly as a result of the rise of non-unionism and the non-union firm. Indeed, the latter may be more a consequence than a cause of the decline of trade unions and collective bargaining.

Notes

1 Had the 1971 Industrial Relations Act remained on the statute book British employers would have enjoyed the means to apply for a ballot to remove bargaining rights from a recognized union under ss. 45–55 (see Dickens and Bain, 1986). Having said this, it is noteworthy that Kochan *et al.*, (1986) do not see the legal provisions concerning certification in the USA as a major factor in the decline of union representation.

2 Unlike 'labour-force density', 'employment density' excludes the unemployed from the denominator, thereby only counting the civilian employed as potential union members. Kelly and Bailey (1989: 56) argue that, since British unions have never sought to organize and represent the unemployed, 'employment density' is a better guide to the extent of workplace trade union membership and union bargaining power with employers.

3 One problem with density estimates based on Department of Employment statistics is that they are derived through reports provided by the trade unions themselves and for a number of reasons – for example, the inclusion of retired members – are widely recognized to be an exaggeration of the actual number of trade union members in employment. A more accurate method is to ask individual employees themselves if they are union members. Since 1989, the British Labour Force Survey has included a question on union membership to individual employees. The 1991 survey suggests that an estimated 9.6 million employees were union members, the lowest figure since 1954 and 25 per cent below the peak levels of 1979, and that employment density was 32 per cent (see Bird *et al.*, 1993).

21

4 For example, firms with high levels of union membership cannot
feasibly deunionize without considerable costs in terms of undermining existing industrial relations and centralized bargaining
structures. Centralization also means that union leaders are in a
position to point these costs out to strategic decision-makers.

2

MANAGEMENT STYLE AND HUMAN RESOURCE MANAGEMENT

The rise of non-unionism and the non-union firm has been closely linked with the emergence of new techniques of human resource management. This issue raises the broader conceptual question of the implications of the absence of trade unions for the management of the employment relationship. As we will see, one assumption concerning HRM is that it acts effectively to 'substitute' for trade unions by reducing employee demands for union services. However, HRM is not the only approach available to management when unions are absent. More traditional tactics of outright opposition might also come to the fore in attempts to avoid unionization.

The aim in this chapter is to review the existing literature on management style or approach in industrial relations. The intention is to identify some conceptual tools to assist in the analysis of our own research findings in subsequent chapters. We will also examine the specific model of management style associated with theories of HRM, and in particular the extent to which it constitutes a non-union model for managing employee relations. We conclude by presenting our own schema for classifying management style in non-union settings and by briefly reviewing existing empirical research on management approach in the absence of unions.

Management style and non-union firms

There have been a number of attempts to develop and refine conceptual models of different styles or approaches to the management of industrial relations. As one might expect, the concern has not been with identifying models of non-union styles alone. Indeed, the principal concern has usually been to identify variations in management approaches between unionized settings.

Most discussions of management style take as their starting point Fox's (1966) distinction between 'unitary' and 'pluralist' views of the employment relationship (see, for example, Purcell and Sisson, 1983; Purcell, 1987; Sisson, 1989a; Marchington and Parker, 1990). Fox identified 'unitary' views as those where trade unions are seen essentially as 'trouble-makers' and 'pluralist' views as those where unions are seen as the legitimate representatives of labour.

In a well-known development of Fox's original formulation, Purcell and Sisson (1983) develop a typology which distinguishes between five different styles or approaches. Three are concerned with management style in unionized settings. Two, though, are derived from a 'unitary' rather than 'pluralist' view of the employment relationship and suggest models of management style appropriate to non-union settings. These are the 'sophisticated paternalist' and 'traditionalist' styles (Sisson, 1989a: 10). In the case of the former, the management objective is to develop policies and practices which make it unnecessary or unattractive for staff to join unions. In the latter case, overt management resistance to unions is coupled with a view of labour as just another factor of production.

In a later work, Purcell provides a development of the original typology in which two separate dimensions of management style are identified. The first is *individualism* – 'the extent to which the firm gives credence to the feelings and sentiments of each employee and seeks to develop and encourage each employee's capacity and role at work' (1987: 536). The second is *collectivism* – 'the extent to which the organisation recognises the right of employees to have a say in those aspects of management decision-making which concern them' (1987: 537). A management whose style emphasizes the value of employees as individuals will focus on them as a resource to be developed and nurtured, while individual relationships between management and employees will involve a strong human relations component. A firm which does not value the individual contribution of its employees will tend to view them as a 'commodity' with little priority given to security of employment and an overt emphasis on direct managerial control and labour costs. In between these two poles is a more paternalistic management style where the emphasis is on 'caring for' rather than 'developing' the human resource.

Firms which recognize their own employees' right to collective representation will regard the existence of democratic structures representing employees as legitimate, or as Purcell (1987: 538) puts it, 'employees have the right to elect some of their number to represent their interests and articulate their views in dialogue with management'. The collective relationship will be seen as *co-operative*, for example where the emphasis is based upon developing constructive relationships in collective bargaining with trade unions; *adversarial*, where the emphasis is placed on collective bargaining as a means of institutionalizing conflict; or *unitary*, where the legitimacy of collective arrangements is called into question by management. The latter would obviously be most likely in non-union settings, or situations where the continuation of union recognition was seriously being questioned by management.

A number of difficulties with the application of Purcell's typology have been identified by Marchington and Parker (1990). They studied management style in four unionized firms. One problem was that the 'resource-status' and 'commodity-status' end-points of the individualism dimension did not in practice appear to be mutually exclusive. Marchington and Parker make the point that when choosing to view labour as a resource, management do not then stop considering it as a cost that has to be controlled. A further problem is that 'individualism' is difficult to identify empirically as a 'discrete aspect of style' in that it is not viewed by management in practice as a separate policy goal distinct from 'collectivism'.

The 'collectivism' dimension is even more problematic (Marchington and Parker, 1990: 235–6). Purcell's original formulation combines both the existence of structures for employee participation (such as collective bargaining) with management approaches to operating these structures. Thus, the more management espouses a commitment to co-operative forms of collective bargaining the further along the collectivism scale it is deemed to be. However, Marchington and Parker (1990: 236) argue that the existence of co-operative collective bargaining and relationships with recognized unions does not mean that management is any more committed to collectivism than if a more adversarial or anti-union approach exists. In all cases, union presence may be a function of the lack of management capacity to resist rather than of its acceptance of the legitimacy of union representation as such. Management may espouse policies which accept the right of employees to independent collective representation but its behaviour may be at variance with this.

The final issue raised by Marchington and Parker concerns the concept of management style itself, especially in the context of the wider notion of management strategy. Purcell (1987: 535) defines 'style' as a corporate steering device that provides 'a distinctive set of guiding principles, written or otherwise, which set parameters and signposts for management action in the way employees are treated and particular events handled'. Marchington and Parker (1990: 232–7) view this as unnecessarily restrictive, focusing upon senior management intentions rather than the actual attitudes and behaviour of management at workplace level. They argue for a wider definition where management style does not have to be conceptualized exclusively at a strategic level but can have 'meaning in all workplaces, irrespective of policy pronouncements', as an influence on the management of employee relations.

In response to these difficulties, Marchington and Parker suggest two alternative dimensions of management style so defined. The first dimension concerns management's approach to employees, that is the extent to which management adopts a 'high' or a 'low' *investment orientation* towards labour. The second dimension concerns management's attitudes and behaviour towards trade unions in the workplace, in particular the extent to which a *partnership orientation* is pursued, rather than an overtly adversarial approach. For Marchington and Parker, the question of whether or not to recognize a union is not important compared to management's behaviour if it is recognized.

We will return to the problem of conceptualizing management style below; suffice it to say that Marchington and Parker's partnership-orientation dimension does not seem particularly applicable to management approaches in non-union settings. However, their observations regarding the meaning of management style do suggest that more attention needs to be given to the strategic dimension of management approach in industrial relations, in particular the relation between corporate intention and the actual practice of line managers at workplace level. This brings us directly to a consideration of new HRM techniques.

HRM and non-union firms

HRM has rapidly become one of the most widely debated and vehemently discussed industrial relations topics in both academic and practitioner circles. This is not surprising since HRM appears to strike at the very core of what the discipline of industrial relations is about, suggesting a broadening beyond, or even a move away from, trade unions and collective bargaining as the main focus of study. Moreover, HRM appears to suggest a more specific academic identification with managerial concerns and interests, shifting the 'natural home' of the study of employee relations from the social science department to the business school.[1] As numerous writers have observed, the debate over HRM has been obscured by the various meanings and definitions, either implicit or explicit, that have been given to the term; an absence of systematic and reliable empirical data; and a tendency for the expression to be used in contradictory and confusing ways (see Guest, 1987; 1989; Storey, 1989; 1992; Legge, 1989; Keenoy, 1990; Blyton and Turnbull, 1993; Clark, 1993).

One problem with the term 'HRM' is that it is not always used to refer to a specific management style or approach. As Storey notes, such 'weak' definitions of HRM tend to be no more than a cosmetic relabelling of what hitherto has been termed in a generic sense 'personnel management'. In other words, HRM is a new and perhaps more 'modern' term for the general activity of managing people in organizations. The real analytical interest in HRM, however, turns on what Storey (1992: 25–6) refers to as 'strong' definitions of the term. It is with HRM in this sense that we are concerned here.

A useful working definition of HRM as a new and distinctive management style is provided by Guest (1987: 509–16). He argues that HRM techniques can be conceptualized as a combination of interdependent personnel policies which are designed to secure the behavioural and attitudinal commitment of employees to the organization and to engender high-quality organizational performance through flexibility and innovation. The policies themselves exhibit *strategic integration*. That is, they are internally coherent, fully integrated with overall corporate business strategy, and provide the framework within which line management makes decisions over personnel issues at workplace level.

From a similar starting point to Guest, Storey (1992: 25) suggests that two different variants of HRM can be identified. The first, or 'soft', version stresses the 'human' aspect of managing human resources. The concerns here are similar to those of 'human relations theory', the objective being to develop managerial strategies which will elicit employee commitment and develop resourceful humans. The second, or 'hard', version is focused on the 'resource' aspect. Here management strategies are designed to optimize the utilization of labour in a dispassionate and formally rational manner. For Storey (1992: 34–6), HRM in both its 'soft' and 'hard' variants has a number of defining characteristics: first, investment in and the development of the human resource is valued as the key to organizational success; second, decisions concerning the human resource are of strategic importance to the organization and are intimately related to the corporate planning process; third, line managers have a key role in the implementation of HRM; and finally, key 'policy levers' are used systematically and in an integrated manner to achieve employee commitment.

This 'ideal-typical' model can be contrasted with the traditional practice of personnel management. Storey (1992: 35) identifies 27 points of difference between personnel management and the theory of HRM. For example, while traditional personnel management is essentially a non-strategic function concerned with formalizing the employment contract, ensuring the consistent application of standard procedure and institutionalizing conflict, the key beliefs and values associated with HRM are those of meeting business needs, securing commitment to the organization's values or 'mission', and 'going beyond' the requirements of the formal employment contract. Similarly, while traditional personnel management views the personnel specialist as the main custodian of policy and practice, HRM emphasizes the key role of line managers.

HRM and trade unions

Is HRM essentially a non-union approach to managing employees? According to Guest, one of the 'organisational pay-offs' from the practice of HRM is allegiance to company rather than union and hence, it could be argued, the enterprise's ability to become or remain non-union. Guest (1989: 43) suggests that the perspectives and values at the core of HRM are unitarist and individualistic, 'leave little scope for collective arrangements and assume little need for collective bargaining. HRM therefore poses considerable challenge to traditional industrial relations and more particularly to trade unionism.' On the other hand, he goes on to argue that HRM is not anti-union in so far as key elements, such as strategic integration and an emphasis on management recognition of the value of employees as humans, are concerned (Guest, 1989: 43).

This point is extended by Storey (1992: 36) who suggests that it may even be debatable to characterize HRM as 'unitarist' since it appears possible that trade unions could be accommodated within the model if a more co-operative relationship is posited. Indeed, Storey's (1992: 243) extensive research in mainstream British organizations in the private and public sector appears to show that 'strong' HRM initiatives can develop in the context of established and well-organized trade union representation – an approach which he terms 'dualism'. However, Storey's qualifications to this conclusion suggest the relationship between HRM initiatives and trade unions is far from complementary. Although, in the firms he studied, the adoption of HRM did not involve an 'overt all-out assault' on trade unions it was also the case that unions did, in most instances, become 'marginalized'.

Product markets, management style and HRM

A number of factors have been suggested as an important influence on the type of approach adopted to the management of employees within organizations. In their original discussion of management styles, Purcell and Sisson (1983: 116–17) concluded that the critical variable was probably the presence of key personalities at early stages in the organization's development. These individuals or family groupings could establish an ethos which came to dominate subsequent development. The growth of many British-owned firms through merger and takeover, however, has tended in many instances to dilute such influences, resulting in opportunistic and pragmatic approaches prevailing in many contemporary organizations. Indeed, this may well be a constraint on the development of full-blown HRM (Purcell, 1989).

More recent discussions of management style, in particular those concerned with HRM, have given particular prominence to the influence of product markets, especially increased product-market competition, as the key contingent factor influencing the type of management style, or acting as a 'trigger' to significant changes in it (Storey, 1992: 44–5; Pettigrew and Whipp, 1991). Having said this, there is little consensus over the precise way in which product markets and management style are related. Some authors have suggested a degree of product-market determinism, at least in the sense that management choices over how to manage labour are subject to limitations imposed by the product-market environment (see, for example, Purcell, 1989). In contrast, others have stressed the power of management to shape the product-market environment or to use product-market conditions as a legitimation for their chosen approach (see, for example, Storey, 1992; and Marchington, 1990, for a review of the literature).

Marchington and Parker (1990: 239–46) provide probably the most sophisticated attempt in the British industrial relations literature to conceptualize the link between product markets and the management of employee relations. As they note, although frequently recognized as a key influence on the way employees are managed, the way in which product markets shape management approaches has usually been hinted at in only superficial terms. They suggest that the power of the product market to influence the way labour is managed is largely shaped by two factors: the degree of competitive pressure and the degree of customer pressure.

The degree of competitive pressure (or degree of monopoly) in the product market measures the extent to which the company can dictate terms to the customer because of the absence of alternative suppliers or, instead, is obliged to follow market trends. Factors such as the ease of market entry will be an important influence on the extent to which a company can establish a monopoly influence. Competitive pressure is likely to be least where demand in the market is growing and other firms find it hard to enter the market, for example because of high capital investment costs. Competitive pressure is likely to be greatest where demand for the company's products is falling and where new competitors can easily enter the market. Under the former situation the product market will exert relatively little pressure on how employee relations are managed and indeed, in more general terms, management will have room for manœuvre in shaping both the market and its responses to it. Under the latter situation the market may be perceived by management as severely limiting, if not determining management actions.

The degree of customer pressure (or degree of monopsony), in the product market is a function of the variability and predictability of customer demand and the structure of the customer profile. The greater the predictability and stability of demand and the more numerous and uncoordinated the customers in the marketplace, the greater the freedom enjoyed by management. Conversely, high levels of unpredictability and variability in a marketplace where there is one large customer purchasing from

31

a range of suppliers, are likely to lead to situations where managements perceive product-market pressures to be determining their actions.

Other factors influencing managerial styles will include the character of the enterprise's product, employee behaviour and, where present, trade union activity. For example, Marchington and Parker suggest that customer pressures may influence not only management style but also employees' behaviour, either through their contacts with customers where their work involves direct contact with them, or more indirectly through their own observations or via management actions designed to create or increase employee awareness of this pressure. The presence of trade unions may also be important in providing a means through which management interpretations of product-market pressures might be challenged, especially where these have been evoked to legitimate their decisions. Interestingly, in non-union environments, they suggest employees may have little scope to challenge managerial interpretations of such market pressures. Where unions are present they, potentially at least, provide an alternative source of information (Marchington and Parker, 1990: 251–2).

The findings of Marchington and Parker's (1990: 252–3) own research suggested that firms experiencing the greatest market pressure were more constrained in their options when it came to choice of management style than those who faced least market pressure. For example, in firms facing low market pressure, there was more scope for management to pursue a partnership approach and a high investment orientation towards employees. Indeed, it has frequently been pointed out that such arch exponents of 'sophisticated paternalism' as IBM and Marks & Spencer can only 'afford' to adopt a high investment approach to their employees precisely because of their dominant product-market position.

HRM and management style in non-union firms

How can existing models of management style be applied to the analysis of industrial relations in non-union settings? Does it make sense, for example, to seek to differentiate management approaches in terms of degrees of individualism and collectivism? Similarly, does the notion of a more strategic approach to the management of employees present a means of distinguishing HRM from traditional personnel management practice?

The research by Marchington and Parker would seem to cast doubt on the extent to which individualism and collectivism, as defined by Purcell, are useful concepts to use in distinguishing management approach. We would suggest that, while not without its difficulties, such a distinction is still meaningful. For example, the problems with the 'individualism' dimension encountered by Marchington and Parker may in part reflect their empirical focus on unionized firms. In any case, we would argue that 'individualism' and 'collectivism' are not mutually exclusive features of management style and, although analytically distinct, are likely both to be present empirically to varying degrees in most circumstances. Indeed, as Marchington and Parker (1990: 80) themselves point out, Purcell's formulation suggests firms may alter their styles along both dimensions at the same time. Thus one would expect a mix of individualism and collectivism that might prove difficult to disentangle empirically.

However, this does not necessarily undermine the analytical usefulness of attempting to locate management styles in terms of the *balance* they seek between the two (Storey and Sisson, 1993). This point is emphasized by Bacon and Storey (1993: 6), who suggest that management may adopt individualist and collectivist approaches in relation to different aspects of the employment relationship depending on whether it is concerned with industrial relations (in its narrow sense), work organization, or human resourcing.

We do agree, however, with Marchington and Parker that it is essential to draw attention to the different levels within an organization at which management style can be articulated, and in particular the importance of the workplace arena in which it is acted out in day-to-day industrial relations. This raises the issue of the relationship between corporate or strategic intentions, the manner in which these may be characterized as a particular 'style' and how they are implemented (or not) lower down the organization. Implicit here is the notion of the extent of 'strategic integration' as a core dimension of management approach which, as we have seen, is a key element in attempts to identify HRM as a distinctive management style.

Thus, we would suggest that in non-union settings it is useful to distinguish between management approaches which exhibit a high degree of strategic integration in the manner implicit in notions of HRM, and those where personnel policy and practice are largely disconnected from business policy and may themselves, in the extreme, lack coherence and formalization. In such circumstances, the approach at workplace level may be largely informal and idiosyncratic and akin to what Brewster and Larsen (1992: 414–15) term a 'Wild West' setting. Here line managers are 'free to develop [their] own style of relationship with employees and, in extreme cases, would have the power to "hire and fire", to reward and to invest in employees as they wished'.

Ambiguities over such a major issue in the employment relationship as whether or not trade unions are compatible with HRM have led critics to argue that the attempt to delineate a new paradigm for managing employees around the concept is flawed. We would suggest that the answer to how far HRM is a means of managing employees without unions may vary according to the particular variant of 'HRM' being dealt with.

For example, Keenoy (1990: 5) identifies two versions of HRM which suggest contrasting positions with regard to trade unions. 'Traditional HRM' has as its basic assumption that 'investment in people is good business if not the basis of good business'. This approach is essentially that identified by Purcell and Sisson as 'sophisticated paternalism' or, in Storey's terms, a 'soft' version of HRM. Here the values of enterprise founders become institutionalized into a particular management style. According to Keenoy, 'traditional HRM' rests on the 'strategic and *philosophical* assumption that recognising and seeking to meet the needs of people leads to a competitive advantage' (emphasis in original). 'Traditional HRM' argues, on the basis of historically founded and deep-seated management values and beliefs, that such investment in human resources should lead to a situation where demands on the part of employees for union services are reduced if not eliminated. If such demands arise, they are a function of managerial failings.

34

A second approach, 'strategic HRM', is viewed by Keenoy as the more novel variant. This approximates to a 'hard' version in Storey's terms. 'Strategic HRM' starts from the question 'what HRM strategy will maximise competitive advantage, optimise control, and minimise unit and labour replacement costs?' (Keenoy, 1990: 5). 'Strategic HRM' assesses the relevance of union presence in terms of contingent factors such as product- and labour-market conditions. If an HRM approach without unions provides the best 'fit' with such contingencies then this should be adopted. Alternatively, if an approach based on collective bargaining provides a better 'fit' then this should prevail (Keenoy, 1990: 6).

Given this, it is important to note that HRM may not involve a rejection of collectivism *per se*. Legge makes this point when she observes that there is in fact a tension in HRM at the normative level: on the one hand, the stress, expressed in management rhetoric, on the relationship between the employer and the employee as an individualized one *and*, on the other, the use in practice of collective forms of work organization or problem-solving (for example, team-working, quality circles). Moreover, such approaches are designed to achieve individual employee commitment to collective organizational goals through the creation of a strong corporate culture that gives 'direction to the organisation' and 'mediates the tension between individualism and collectivism, as individuals socialised into a strong culture are subject to unobtrusive collective controls on attitudes and behaviour' (Legge, 1989: 35–6).

Rather than a rejection of collectivism therefore, it may be that form of collectivism which is embodied in the independent representation of employee interests by trade unions and collective bargaining that is being called into question. Thus HRM would be perfectly consistent with either overtly individual or (non-union) collective regulation (for example, through the use of company councils – see Incomes Data Services, 1989), although Legge's analysis is that the device of a strong corporate culture is used to mask the use of collective controls by presenting the employment relationship in individualized terms. This could mean that HRM approaches may well emerge in unionized settings and coexist alongside collective bargaining – as Storey's observation of 'dualism' in unionized British organizations, noted earlier, implies. However, where this does occur, union organization and collective bargaining of an adversarial kind stand to be significantly modified as a condition of their long-term survival.

In sum, we suggest that management style in non-union settings can usefully be explored along two dimensions: first, the degree of 'strategic integration' between individual personnel policies and between these and overall business strategy; second, the *balance* between individual and collective methods of regulation in relation to particular substantive and procedural aspects of the employment relationship. HRM-type approaches would be those which exhibit high levels of strategic integration, and the variant most likely to be associated with non-union status would be 'traditional HRM', although non-unionism may occur as a result of the adoption of 'strategic HRM'.

Empirical research on management style in non-union firms

Finally, it is important to note the findings of the small amount of existing empirical research on management style in non-union firms. The only really extensive and detailed academic study of management policies in the large non-union firm is provided by Foulkes (1980). He studied 26 large non-union firms in the USA (the majority had over 10,000 employees). All but three operated in manufacturing, many were in 'high-technology' growth sectors and all but six appeared in the *Fortune 500* list of top performing corporations in 1975. Foulkes's findings would appear to provide a classic empirical statement of 'traditional HRM' or 'sophisticated paternalism' in practice – for example, company values were 'people-centred' and often influenced by founders' ideas; personnel policies were designed to foster employee commitment and involvement; and the personnel function played a key strategic role.

A not dissimilar characterization is gleaned by Beaumont (1987: 117–30) from his review of mainly journalistic and prac-titioner accounts of the practices of household-name non-union firms in Britain such as IBM, Marks & Spencer and Gillette. Again, an emphasis on achieving strong organizational commitment and a pronounced tendency to view the employee as an individual were prominent. Of course, such similarities may reflect the fact that many of the household-name non-union firms operating in Britain are, in fact, American-owned. This suggests that personnel policies and practices may be systematically transplanted from the USA (Beaumont and Townley, 1985; see also Buckley and Enderwick, 1985). It has also been suggested that this approach may also be particularly prevalent in 'high-technology' industries where US firms may have a particular influence (Cressey, 1985; Cressey *et al.*, 1985; Beaumont, 1986; Kleingartner and Anderson, 1987).

Aside from being associated with foreign ownership and sectors such as 'high technology', non-unionism has largely been seen as a small-enterprise phenomenon on the grounds that small firms are far more likely to be non-union than are large firms. Indeed, most of the academic research on non-unionism in Britain has been undertaken under the 'small business' rubric (see Curran, 1991, for a review), and there is a case for suggesting that small firms might be a better guide to the source of 'role models' for larger British-owned enterprises than the approach of foreign-owned firms operating in Britain. For example, Goss (1991b: 153) notes that British government policies towards labour-market deregulation are based on an image of small firms as 'prime examples of the benign and beneficial effects of greater individualisation' and an assumption that 'the small-firm model' is one which can and should be emulated by larger enterprises.

However, small business researchers have suggested a more complex model of the management of small-firm employment relations. For example, Goss (1991a: 75–9) distinguishes a variety of management approaches according to the extent of the employer's economic dependence on employees and the ability of employees to resist the exercise of the employer's prerogative. These include 'fraternalism', where the employer is highly dependent upon the skills of the employee, and labour management is more a matter of negotiation between the employer as a 'colleague' and relatively powerful workers; 'paternalism', where employer dependence on employees is less marked and the power of employees lower, enabling the employer to cultivate strong identification among employees; 'benevolent autocracy', where the employer's position of power is clearly established but employees are not so dependent on the employer that they cannot assert some degree of independence, and hence the employment relationship 'combines in a vital tension cordial and particularistic employer–employee interactions with the impersonal dictates of market forces'; and 'sweating', where the dominant employer treats weak employees as a commodity to be controlled according to market requirements.

While we are not concerned with employment relations in small enterprises as such in this book, it is important to recognize that they may provide a useful reference point when it comes to considering larger non-union enterprises. The findings of the 1990 WIRS on management attitudes to unions in non-union establishments (36 per cent of the overall sample) provide interesting food for thought on this point. The survey revealed that management attitudes were only 'hostile' to unions in just under one-third of workplaces. Having said that, they were only 'in favour' of unions in 2 per cent of cases, the vast majority declaring themselves 'neutral' on the matter. What appeared to be linked to hostility to trade unions was whether the establishment was part of a larger enterprise. Where this was the case, then hostility was more likely. This, the survey authors concluded, 'is suggestive of a general management policy of union avoidance in some larger organisations' and not 'a widespread anti-union stance among smaller firms' (Millward *et al.*, 1992: 70).

Conclusion

Our concern in this chapter has been to draw out those aspects of the debate concerning the analysis and explanation of management approaches and style which are of relevance to the study of industrial relations in non-union settings. In particular, we have suggested that a distinction between individualism and collectivism on the one hand, and the degree of strategic integration on the other, may be useful in analysing management approaches in non-union settings. At the same time, an awareness of product-market pressures may be important in understanding the scope management has to choose between particular styles.

The concept of HRM has particular analytical significance in non-union settings. First, a key defining characteristic of HRM is high levels of strategic integration. Second, although not necessarily incompatible with trade union presence, it is based on a unitary model of the enterprise. Trade unions and collective bargaining appear particularly difficult to accommodate with some variants of HRM. Our review of the existing research suggested that non-union management styles in practice tend towards 'traditional HRM' in sectors such as 'high technology' and are linked to a strategic orientation and a high level of individualization of the employment relationship. However, we also noted other less strategically-integrated approaches, especially among smaller non-union firms. Our review of existing research suggested that in practice non-union management styles tend towards 'traditional HRM' in sectors such as 'high technology' and are strongly linked to a strategic orientation and a high level of individualization of the employment relationship. However, we also noted other less strategically integrated management approaches, especially among smaller non-union firms. We will explore variations in management style in non-union enterprises in the context of our own data in the following two chapters.

Note

1 See the debate between Dunn (1990; 1991) and Keenoy (1991) on the implications of the 'new' industrial relations and 'HRM' for the 'old' industrial relations.

3

NON-UNIONISM AND MANAGEMENT STYLE IN 'HIGH TECH'

In this chapter we begin our exploration of non-union employee relations based on the results of the empirical study outlined in our Introduction. Our concern here and in the following chapter is with the characteristics of management style in settings where unions are absent. In this chapter we explore the issue through the results of our postal and follow-up interview surveys in establishments in the 'high-technology' sector in the South East of England. As we have noted already, this sector and geographical area is associated with disproportionate levels of non-unionism, while in particular those that are US-owned computing and electronics companies are frequently seen as leading exponents of new HRM techniques. Our main objective, therefore, is to explore the extent to which non-unionism in the establishments studied was associated with management styles of an HRM type. In order to assess this, and the character of other management approaches that may be evident, we will employ the concepts of 'strategic integration' and 'individualism/ collectivism' outlined in the previous chapter. We begin, however, with the question of the extent of non-unionism in the high-technology sector.

Non-unionism in the high-technology sector

According to some commentators the high-technology sector is virtually a 'no-go' area for trade unions (see, for example, Bassett, 1986). This view is changed by Sproull and MacInnes who in two surveys of the Scottish electronics industry conducted in the 1980s, found that six out of ten employees worked in organizations where unions were recognized and four out of ten employees were trade union members (Sproull and MacInnes, 1987; 1989). However, a more recent survey, also conducted in Scotland, suggested that the industry had significantly lower levels of union density than manufacturing as a whole, and that the concentration of employment growth in non-union establishments was acting further to dilute union density (Findlay, 1992: 64–5; 1993: 30).

One problem with such findings is the rather narrow and imprecise definition of the 'high technology' sector used (Beaumont, 1986). In particular, studies by industrial relations researchers tend to focus on the electronics or computing industries (see, for example, Sproull and MacInnes, 1987; 1989; Causer and Jones, 1992; Findlay, 1992; 1993). Beaumont (1986) argues for a broader definition such as the 'official' definition given in Butchart (1987). This includes a wider range of industries such as pharmaceuticals as well as electronics and computing'.

Adopting this broader definition survey in the South East of England[2] revealed establishments in the high-technology sector so defined to be markedly non-union, both in terms of recognition and membership density.[3] Eighty per cent of establishments did not recognize trade unions, under half of employees were employed in establishments where unions were recognized (see Table 3.1), and, by our estimate, only one in ten employees were union members. Moreover, non-union establishments were associated with employment growth and union recognition with employment decline or static employment levels. It is also worth noting that only a tiny minority of establishments had experienced union-organizing attempts during the 1980s, although conversely very few had engaged in union derecognition.

As we noted in the previous chapter, one factor that has frequently been alluded to in attempts to explain non-unionism,

Table 3.1   Union recognition in the postal survey sample

Employee categories for which unions recognized	Percentage of establishments	Percentage of employees
No unions	80	54
Manual and non-manual	12	34
Manual only	7	11
Non-manual	1	1

especially in the high-technology sector, is the presence of foreign-owned firms, especially from the USA. In fact one in three employees in our survey was employed in US-owned firms. Surprisingly, Sproull and MacInnes's surveys could find no statistical relationship between ownership and non-union status. Instead, they pointed to the size and age of establishments and whether 'single-status' arrangements existed for all employees, as the key factors determining recognition. Our postal survey broadly replicated these findings so far as the relationship of recognition to size and age were concerned (we did not enquire about the presence of 'single-status' arrangements in the postal survey); however, we found that larger US establishments (that is, those with 500 or more employees) were more likely to be non-union than their British counterparts (see Table 3.2). It was also the case that over half of the new establishments founded in the 1980s were made up of US- and other foreign-owned firms.

There was also an indication from our survey of a relatively high prominence being given to personnel issues which might be taken as a (very) crude indicator of the practice of HRM. In all, responsibility for personnel or industrial relations matters was the province of an individual with a 'personnel' job title (usually 'personnel manager' or 'personnel director') in well over half of establishments. Moreover, while an on-site personnel specialist was no more likely to be present in the US-owned establishments than British- or other foreign-owned establishments, where they

Table 3.2 Establishment characteristics and union recognition in the postal survey sample

Establishment characteristic	Establishments with recognition		Employees at establishments with recognition	
	No.	%	No.	%
Employment size				
90–199	9	31	1059	36
200–499	8	26	2799	29
500+	6	43	9660	62
Date establishment founded in UK				
Pre-1950	5	62	3950	73
1950s	4	36	3428	65
1960s	5	28	3980	57
1970s	4	27	714	18
1980s	5	8	1446	19
Ownership				
British	8	23	7041	58
US	7	20	4890	65
Other foreign	4	33	1187	54
British independent	4	12	400	9
All establishments	23	20	13,518	44

N = 115 (30,553 employees)

were present in US-owned cases they were likely to spend more time on personnel matters and to be better qualified.

However, notwithstanding the apparent significance given to personnel matters, and the influence of US ownership, overall our findings would suggest that factors other than HRM might be more important in explaining the predominance of non-unionism. For example, most establishments in the survey were young (just over half were set up during the 1980s); often had workforces where technical occupations without a strong tradition of trade union organization were in the majority; tended to be relatively small in terms of the numbers employed at the surveyed location; and had not been targeted by unions for recruitment. In short, the absence of unions could be taken more as a function of the immaturity of the establishments, the composition of their workforces, and the particular economic and political conditions during the 1980s which had discouraged union-organizing attempts, than the practice of US-derived HRM. However, in order to explore this suggestion in more depth we need to examine management style and the policies and practices which might underpin it. We now turn, therefore, to our follow-up interview survey.

Management style in non-union settings

The follow-up interview establishments were selected, as far as was possible, to be representative of the larger postal survey. Out of the 30 establishments selected and who agreed to participate further, 23 turned out to have no recognized unions present (see Table 3.3). Of these, 19 establishments were part of larger organizations which did not recognize unions elsewhere in their operations. The remaining four organizations recognized unions for at least one category of employee (manual, white-collar or professional/managerial). Of the seven establishments with recognized unions present, in only one case were unions recognized for all categories of employee both at the establishment and in the company as a whole. The other establishments were equally divided between those that recognized unions for only one category of employee and were part of larger organizations which did not recognize unions elsewhere, and those which had recognition for one category of employees and were part of a firm which similarly recognized unions for some elements of its workforce elsewhere. In what follows we are mainly concerned with management style in the 23 non-union establishments. However, the partial coverage of union recognition in all but one of the remaining establishments indicates that some consideration of these cases is also warranted.

44

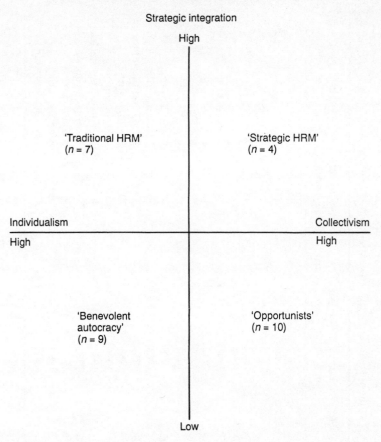

Figure 3.1 Management styles in the follow-up survey establishments

Overall, our findings suggested that a distinctive clustering of management styles could be identified among the 30 establishments. Management approaches at seven (23 per cent) of the establishments were categorized as *traditional HRM* (high strategic integration/high individualization) ; four (13 per cent) as *strategic HRM* (high strategic integration/high collectivization); a further nine (30 per cent) as *benevolent autocracy* (low strategic integration/high individualization); and ten (30 per cent) as *opportunists* (low strategic integration/high collectivization) (see Figure 3.1).

Table 3.3 Profile of the follow-up survey establishments

Company	Ownership	Date founded in Britain	Unions recognized	Employment at establishment	Main activity at establishment
Consumer Electronics	UK	1972	No	250	Manufacturing
Computer Supplier	US	1988	No	200	Marketing & Customer Support
Pharmaceuticals	US	1957	Yes	1800	Sales & Manufacture
R & D Laboratory	UK	1962	No	800	R & D
Electrical Equipment	US	1984	Yes	400	Manufacture
R & D Laboratory	UK	1952	No	390	R & D
R & D Laboratory	UK	1979	No	90	R & D
Research Laboratory	UK	1946	No	220	R & D
Consumer Electronics	UK	1988	No	500	Manufacturing
Electrical Controls	US	1963	No	950	Manufacturing
Electrical Equipment	UK	1955	No	500	R & D and Manufacture
Electrical Equipment	US	1984	No	130	Manufacturing
Medical Equipment	US	1980	No	410	Manufacturing
Electrical Controls	UK	1971	Yes	400	Design & Manufacture
Electrical Equipment	US	1983	No	500	Manufacturing
Consumer Electronics	UK	1961	Yes	300	Manufacturing
Electronics	US	1963	No	280	Manufacturing
Electronics	Japan	1988	No	300	Sales & Marketing

Company	Ownership	Date founded in Britain	Unions recognized	Employment at establishment	Main activity at establishment
Medical Equipment	UK	1984	No	290	Design & Manufacture
Medical Equipment	UK	1982	No	180	R & D and Manufacture
Electronics	Japan	1983	No	210	Sales & Marketing
R & D Laboratory	UK	1972	No	350	Development
Advanced Materials	UK	1946	No	1000	Manufacture
Electrical Equipment	UK	1970	No	230	R&D/Manufacture
Aerospace Equipment	US	1957	Yes	1200	Manufacture
Computer Services	UK	1968	Yes	280	Software Service
Computer Peripherals	US	1986	No	100	Marketing & Customer Support
Computer Supplier	US	1969	No	400	Marketing & Customer Support
Pharmaceuticals	UK	1889	Yes	3000	Manufacturing
Computer Peripherals	UK	1971	No	170	Manufacturing

As one would expect, high levels of individualization were strongly associated with non-union status. All but one of the establishments where individual rather than collective modes of job regulation were dominant were non-union *and* part of a non-union firm. Conversely, again as one might expect, high levels of collectivization were less likely to be associated with non-union status, although seven out of the 14 establishments here still did not recognize unions. This underlines the point that it is the *balance* between individualism and collectivism that is important when considering management style and that the absence of unions does not in itself preclude some elements of a collective approach to managing aspects of the employment relationship. Significantly, the level of strategic integration did not appear to be strongly related to the presence or absence of unions, suggesting that, in itself, an HRM-type approach was not inevitably associated with non-union status. We will now examine the four management styles identified in more detail.

'Traditional HRM'

Management approaches exhibiting high levels of strategic integration and high individualization can be regarded as *variations* on what was identified in Chapter 2 as 'traditional HRM'. It will be recalled that this referred to a management style where human resources are seen as central to achieving the objectives of the enterprise, in that recognizing and seeking to meet the *individual* needs of employees is assumed to be a source of competitive advantage. One consequence of this is assumed to be a low level of demand for union services. This managerial style is therefore not overtly anti-union but likely to point, at least in the minds of managers, to the irrelevance of trade unions to employees who are being managed effectively as individuals.

In nearly all cases, establishments where the management approach was placed in this category had a predominantly white-collar and professional workforce and did not carry out manufacturing or assembly operations (although some did at other sites) (see Table 3.4). They also tended to be younger establishments, four out of the seven having been established

Table 3.4 Characteristics of the follow-up survey
establishments by management style type

	Style type				
	Trad. HRM	Strat. HRM	Benev. autoc.	Opportunists	Totals
Number of cases	7	4	9	10	30
No recognized union	7	0	9	7	23
Part of non-union firm	6	0	9	4	19
Foreign-owned	4	3	4	2	13
Under 300 employees	2	0	7	4	13
Under 20% manual employees	6	0	2	4	12
Founded since 1979	4	2	3	3	12
Manufacturing and/or assembly undertaken	1	4	7	7	19

since 1979. Four of the establishments were foreign-owned, two
by American corporations and two by Japanese multinationals.

The strategic orientation of management policies was evi-
denced in a number of ways. For example the presence of a
personnel director in the firm, the existence of formal statements
of employment philosophy and early personnel management
involvement in change programmes. In one case a US-owned
computer peripherals sales and service establishment with 200
employees, the personnel director emphasized that the human
resources function was orientated towards 'strategic thinking'
rather than 'personnel administration', and a key objective was
to maintain the company reputation in the locality as a 'high-
quality' employer. Human resource considerations were seen as
central to the strategic planning process and the personnel
director himself played a leading role in drafting the UK

operation's strategic business plan for the next five years. Involvement in this process enabled particular human resource issues which would follow from planned product innovations to be highlighted. These included a problem of skills redundancy and a requirement for a shift in skill base of the workforce from hardware to software skills.

In all cases management claimed to have always placed a strong emphasis on the effective management of people as a key to good business practice. However, for some, this long-standing concern had gained a renewed and more strategic emphasis in recent years as a consequence of attempts to adapt to new environmental pressures and business circumstances. For example, in three (all British-owned) cases this had meant an increase in the importance of the personnel function in developing integrated personnel policies and in linking these to the new directions in business policies. In one example, a research and development laboratory was faced with a decline in government defence contracts and demands for increased profitability from the British parent company. It therefore had to seek new markets by offering its consultancy services on a commercial basis to the aerospace and defence industries. For the personnel specialism this had meant an increased role in a number of areas, particularly line-management training and development to emphasize the importance of 'people management' as a key element of more cost-effective project management; the management of remuneration policies to attract employees with scarce software skills; and the retraining of the existing workforce to maximize the marketability of its expertise.

High individualization in managing the employment relationship in the establishments in this category was emphasized through policy devices such as single-status terms and conditions, employee profit-sharing and share-ownership schemes, performance-related pay (especially where a relatively high proportion of individual increases were determined by this means) and, in some cases, the explicit linking of individual appraisal schemes to pay determination. In addition, there was usually a strong emphasis placed on employee training and development in which the appraisal process (in the two Japanese-owned firms this took the form of 'self-appraisal') played an important role. Viewing employees as 'individuals' was normally seen to pay explicit dividends for the company.

In most cases relatively sophisticated non-union voice mechanisms were also present. Two of the three British companies had a staff committee with elected employee representatives, and in all cases a degree of prominence was given to direct communications with employees. This included deliberate attempts to maximize the free flow of information vertically through the management chain and horizontally across functions through such devices as briefing groups, employee attitude surveys and workforce meetings. In one case, an annual company meeting was held where all employees and their spouses were lodged at the firm's expense in a country hotel in order to hear reports from senior mangers on business performance and future plans.

In some establishments the managers interviewed explained their non-union status explicitly in terms of the alternative means they had established to manage employees. In one of the British-owned companies it was argued, for example, that there was 'no need' for a trade union because deliberate attempts were made to substitute for trade union presence.

> Unions have a positive role in that they tend to make you make your mind up more quickly, and to conform to procedures rather more diligently. We do a number of things which hopefully ensure that the functions of unions are carried out . . . (Personnel manager, electrical company)

In other instances non-union status was also explained as a consequence of the company responding to the need to offer superior terms and conditions of employment in order to recruit and retain highly-skilled technical and professional employees in competitive labour-market conditions. As our interviewee in a Japanese electronics company put it: 'the underlying philosophy here is that if we try to keep our terms and conditions competitive and we look after people, there should, hopefully, be no reason for a union to emerge'.

Elsewhere, in the context of a labour-shedding and restructuring exercise by a US office supplier of office computer systems, management claimed that employees saw no need for unions.

Indeed, the absence of unions was not seen by our interviewees as a result of explicit management policy (the majority of board members were said to be supporters of the Labour Party!) but as a simple reflection of the absence of any need for them when rewards were high, working conditions good, and even the redundancy package 'generous'. In general working for the company was described as 'fun, frustrating . . . better to do and get it wrong than not to do . . . thriving on chaos'.

A common theme was that if any demands for union services were to arise, this would be seen as a product of managerial failings. For example, the personnel manager in a research and development laboratory commented:

> We feel that there is no interest in unions on either side . . .
> We will be non-unionized just as long as the quality of management deserves it. As soon as it falls below a certain level or standard we will have unions in.

Such views were strongly underpinned by unitary values, the most explicit expression of which was found in one of the Japanese-owned establishments. The company had a rather philosophical (if not spiritual!) statement of its seven basic values and a 'code of conduct' was displayed, we were told, in every office in the organization. For example, under the heading 'Harmony and Co-operation', it was stated:

> Alone we are weak, together we are strong. We shall work together as a family in mutual trust and responsibility. An association of talented men is but an unruly mob unless each member is imbued with this spirit.

However, in both this and the other Japanese establishment, it was clear that British managers adopted a more pragmatic stance than their Japanese superiors. For example, in one of them, the task for the British management team was seen as to 'mix and match' Japanese employment philosophies with British custom and practice. One illustration of this was the company approach to union recognition, where unions were recognized for all employees in the industrial division (there was no distinction between manual and white-collar staff) but not among staff in the sales and marketing divisions.

In the other case, a 1200-strong British workforce was not unionized, apparently deliberately so. When an attempt to organize at one of the firm's two Scottish manufacturing plants was made, this was resisted. According to the British personnel and administration manager we interviewed, this was because the Japanese had 'a great reluctance to deal with a union because it is alien to their way of doing business' and were 'shocked' that employees felt they needed to 'evoke a third party'. British managers in the company, on the other hand, had taken a more pragmatic view and saw unions as 'a rather unfortunate fact of life and something that has got to be managed positively'.

A further reason for the absence of unions given in these and many of the other establishments was the nature of the workforce itself. As noted above, this tended to be entirely white-collar and professional or, at the least, contained a very high proportion of such workers. Given such a composition, managers claimed that unions were seen by all concerned as irrelevant. For example, in an electrical equipment company, lack of interest on the part of both the workforce and management was seen as the main reason for union absence. According to the personnel manager, '"union" is a word that is just not talked about on this site'. Finally, having given examples of the high level of commitment among employees, the personnel director of the US-owned computer peripherals establishment cited earlier, commented that unions had nothing to offer either employer or employee: 'I'm not sure what they would bring to the party is the honest answer.'

'Benevolent autocracy'

In Chapter 2 we also referred to a management style, 'benevolent autocracy', identified in small business research by Goss (1991a; 1991b). Here the employer's position of power is clearly established in relation to employees but, by virtue of their skills or competencies, they are not entirely dependent upon the employer and can exert a degree of labour-market independence. As a result, management approaches to employee relations seek to foster a close identification between the employee and the enterprise. This goes beyond paternalism but is not manifested in a full-blown strategy as implied by an HRM-type approach. The management styles in the follow-up survey which exhibited a high degree of individualization but low degree of strategic integration, appear broadly to fit this notion. Notably, it was frequently associated with the small-firm origins of the establishments, which were often still reflected in establishment size (most establishments in this category had under 300 employees). It can also be noted that, in contrast to the establishments where 'traditional HRM' was predominant, a significant proportion of the workforce in each of these establishments were manual employees and that, in all but two cases, manufacturing and/or assembly took place at the site.

In these cases, personnel policies and practice showed a low level of strategic integration with overall business policy and in some cases a low level of integration with each other. In some instances individual policies were poorly developed or did not exist and, in others, there was no personnel specialist on the site, or the post had only recently been created. A low priority tended to be given to training and development, or if it was prioritized, it tended to be focused on technical training rather than managerial skills and development. None of these establishments recognized trade unions and all were part of a non-union firm. As such, a relatively high level of individualization of the employment relationship was in evidence in relation to questions of pay determination, consultation and performance appraisal and so on. Grievance handling also tended to be conducted through the management chain, and information provision through a variety of *ad hoc* mechanisms such as occasional managing director briefings or the use of electronic mail, although in three cases an elected staff consultative committee also existed. In the main, the absence of unions was not a product of overtly expressed deep-seated anti-union values on the part of management. Rather, in most instances the issue appeared to never have arisen and no formal stance towards trade unions had ever been formulated.

An illustration of this approach is provided by two separate divisions of the same parent company, all of whose operations were located in and around a university town. The parent company had been founded in the 1950s by an academic at the university who began operations from a caravan in his garden. There were now five operating divisions which had been set up over time to exploit particular product innovations. The companies were mostly concerned with the research, development and manufacture of health-care and electronics products. The operating companies enjoyed a high degree of autonomy and the group headquarters had a small staff of under 20 employees. Although each individual company had developed its own variation on the original ethos, the influence of the founder was still strong throughout the group. The most important principle was seen to be to keep operating companies small (around 300 employees was seen as the maximum) in order to provide a 'more human' and 'small company' working environment which would stimulate and reward innovation. As one of our interviewees said of the approach: 'the philosophy is keep it small and maintain this image of caring'.

The group as a whole did not have a personnel director, and formally no group-wide personnel policy-making took place, although personnel managers at the various companies did meet frequently. In both the establishments we studied personnel policies and practices were relatively formalized, although at one of the sites there was no specialist personnel manager. In fact the personnel manager had recently left and it had been decided there was insufficient work to justify appointing a replacement. Personnel was therefore now the responsibility of the financial controller. At the site where a personnel specialist was present, her role appeared to be mainly administrative and not to involve extensive involvement in policy-making. The absence of unions in the operating companies and the group as a whole seemed to be more a matter of accident than design; as one of our interviewees put it, 'frankly it is because we've never been approached'.

The other establishments in this category again represented variations on the theme. For example, an electronics company had recently been taken over by an American company. The new parent was encouraging a 'more open' approach to managing employees. One reason for this was the tight labour-market conditions that the establishment faced, and the need for it to be able to recruit and retain employees with skills required by new product developments. Here, therefore, it was the case that a 'benevolent' approach was in the process of being adopted. Again, union organization had never been an issue in the company, which was founded in 1957.

Other establishments in this category also provided evidence of an increased importance being attached to 'people' matters within the context of a more 'benevolent' approach. In the case of a British-owned establishment manufacturing computer terminals and workstations, for example, a change in management approach involved the creation of a personnel function. In most of these cases non-union status once more appeared to be more of an 'accident' than a conscious choice and was said to be an issue that employees had never raised.

'Opportunists'

In this group of establishments the management approach exhibited fragmented personnel policies and practices which, as in the cases just described, sometimes lacked formalization. In some instances 'people' issues were given a low priority and training and development were often minimal. However, unlike the 'benevolent autocrat' approach, the regulation of the employment relationship usually involved a higher level of collectivization.

In three of the ten cases, unions had been derecognized during the 1980s but a predominantly collective approach retained; in four others, unions had always been absent from the establishment (although in some instances present in the company of which the establishment was a part); and in three further cases, unions were recognized, but only for one element of the workforce. In their various ways managements in all these establishments tended to be reactive and opportunistic in their response to circumstances, although a marked degree of hostility to unions was sometimes evident in managerial utterances. Personnel specialists, where they were present, often acted in an administrative or 'conflict-management' capacity. Overall, the management style in most of these cases is probably best regarded as a 'non-union variation' on the theme of the 'standard modern' or 'fire-fighting' approach identified as typical of larger

British-owned manufacturing firms (Purcell and Sisson, 1983). Indeed, the majority of establishments had over 300 employees, had a significant proportion of manual employees, were engaged in manufacturing and/or assembly at the site, and were in all but two cases British-owned.

In the cases where unions had been derecognized the decision was said to have been a response to a fall-off in union membership. For example, in one case, a British independent consumer electronics firm, the TGWU had won recognition in the mid-1970s but this had lapsed at the end of the decade. Rather than attribute it to deliberate policy, management blamed declining union membership among employees on the effects of recession. However, a company council had been introduced by management in 1976 and, in the absence of union representation, this was now deemed to satisfy many of the functions that a union might perform.

In four further establishments, unions had never been recognized. In three cases the establishments concerned were companies owned by much larger UK multi-divisional enterprises (although one had just been acquired by a major German firm) whose other divisions, usually involved in manufacturing, recognized trade unions. In the case of the particular divisions in which our establishments were located, the staff concerned were normally predominantly professional or technical employees. They were usually employed in R&D or computing functions, and historically had not been organized to the extent that recognition had been sought. For example, in the computer services bureau of a large manufacturing company whose main activity lay outside the computing industry, some attempts to recruit by ASTMS had occurred in the past but had not resulted in a recognition claim. It was reported that establishment management was 'neutral' on the question of recognition.

The fourth establishment was a British-owned independent consumer electronics company. Despite being described as 'classic T&G country' by the personnel manager, there was no history of union recruitment activity reported. Neither, according to the personnel manager, would it have been welcome: 'perish the thought of any of that coming here because we're quite happy without it'.

Finally, it is worth noting that in the three establishments where unions were recognized for at least one category of employee, the extent of union influence had gradually been eroded during the 1980s, not least as individual members left or new recruits to the enterprise failed to join. For example, at one establishment producing image-processing equipment, unions were recognized for only manual employees, who constituted just over one-third of the 230-strong workforce. It was also reported that union membership among this group had been in decline during the 1980s and, although there was no explicit management policy to deunionize, unions were regarded as becoming increasingly irrelevant to the task of managing employee relations. In another case, a US-owned manufacturer of electrical equipment, the AEU was recognized for the manual workforce, which constituted about half of total employees. However, union influence had again been in decline over a period of years. Members had been lost during a period of contentious industrial action, a closed-shop agreement had ceased, and a leading shop steward had been sacked. At the time of our contact with the establishment, union bargaining rights were limited to assembly workers, while skilled craft grades had been placed on 'staff' status, although the union retained representation rights.

'Strategic HRM'

The final category of management styles we identified was 'strategic HRM'. The first point to note here is that all four establishments included here recognized trade unions for significant elements, but by no means all, of their workforce. In fact, these establishments tended to be larger and included in their ranks the two largest in the follow-up survey. They also had a large proportion of manual employees among the workforce and all carried out manufacturing and/or assembly operations. Three out of four of these establishments were American-owned, although in one case this was the result of a recent takeover.

Our interest in these unionized establishments is twofold. First, they provide a further example of a strategic approach to managing employee relations of an HRM-type. Second, and more important, they allow us to throw some light on the issue of the extent to which HRM is an exclusively non-union approach to managing employee relations. As we noted in Chapter 2, 'strategic HRM' revolves around the notion of achieving a tight integration between business and human resource policy and practice in order to secure better utilization of labour. The precise form of management approach is therefore contingent upon what is perceived as providing the 'best fit' with overall business objectives in order to maximize competitive advantage, optimize control and minimize labour costs. Thus, high levels of collectivization, including union recognition, are likely to be perceived to suit some circumstances. Equally, increased individualization, and derecognition of unions, could be seen as a strategic adjustment to improve the 'degree of fit' where such circumstances are perceived to have radically altered.

A strategic orientation in these four cases was exhibited in much the same way as described previously. The balance between individual and collective regulation of the employment relationship was, however, weighted more towards the latter. In some cases, though, an *increased* individualization of hitherto predominantly collective employment relations as part of a strategic response to new competitive conditions and/or business circumstances was in process.

For example, in one establishment which formed the main British site of a US-owned pharmaceutical multinational, a major expansion programme was in progress, with particular emphasis being placed on improving 'time to market' while remaining highly competitive in terms of quality and price. Human resources were seen as the key to the success of these plans. Numerous change initiatives were in train, including Total Quality Management, the introduction of a new grade of 'team leader' and 'performance counselling' on the shop floor. Particular emphasis was being placed by the company on developing a 'system of trust' whereby change would be readily accepted by the workforce. At the same time, a more individualized approach on key issues such as pay determination was favoured, especially for the white-collar workforce. Although four manual and two white-collar unions were represented at the establishment, only the manual union enjoyed full recognition. Significant changes in relationships with the white-collar unions were reported where, it was claimed, employee support had more or less collapsed. Moreover, this was seen as a direct result of 'enlightened management' whereby employees were now treated 'as people' rather than as 'union members'.

Similar trends were evident in a second case where a takeover by an American company had led to the introduction of a new 'company employment philosophy' aimed at 'unlocking the best' in each individual employee and rewarding 'excellence'. Tangible policy innovations that had accompanied this initiative included profit-sharing and share-ownership schemes open to all grades of staff. While the existing status of the trade unions had not been challenged, the senior personnel and training manager interviewed confided that some members of the management team favoured their marginalization or even derecognition.

In contrast, the two other establishments in this category suggested that a strategic approach does not necessarily mean a reduction in the role of trade unions. For example, following an employee ballot, one company had extended full recognition to cover scientific and technician staff in the mid-1980s and, at the same time, the bargaining agenda had been extended to cover issues such as paternity breaks and career breaks for female employees. The management described its relationship with the unions as co-operative and as an integral feature of its approach.

Management style, product markets and other environmental pressures

As we noted in Chapter 2, considerable analytical stress has been placed in recent years on the importance of the link between management style and product-market conditions. Moreover, HRM has been viewed as an approach which purports to make the link between such factors in management practice more explicit. To what extent were the management styles found in the follow-up survey establishments related to particular product-market and other environmental pressures or contingent factors?

While our data from the follow-up survey allow only a superficial classification,[4] very few of the establishments appeared to

Table 3.5   Extent of product-market pressure in the follow-up
survey establishments

Product-market pressure	No.	%
Very high	1	3
High	11	37
Some	9	30
Low	7	23
Very low	2	7

Note:
Very high = declining demand for product + easy market entry for new
competitors + unpredictable customer demands + narrow customer base.
Very low = increasing demand for product + difficult market entry for
competitors + predictable customer demands + wide customer base.

be experiencing very high or very low product-market pressures
in the manner defined by Marchington and Parker (1990) (see
Table 3.5). About a third appeared to be experiencing relatively
high pressure, a further third some more limited pressure in the
form of competitive or customer pressures, or a mix of both, and
just over a fifth relatively low product-market pressure. The first
point to make is that there appeared to be no clear relationship in
our follow-up survey between the level of product-market
pressure and the four broad clusters of management approaches
we identified. This should not be surprising since the logic of
Marchington and Parker's model is to identify the extent to which
these factors act as a constraint on, or are perceived as a
determinant of, management actions. It does not suggest that
particular approaches to industrial relations are determined by,
or can be 'read off' from, the degree of power exerted by the
market.

   Another way of looking at this issue in the context of our data is
to ask to what extent the management approach to industrial
relations, regardless of type, was perceived by management to be
a reflection of product-market constraints. In this respect, it
seemed clear that in many cases sufficient freedom from adverse
competitive and strong customer pressure existed to allow for
a reasonable amount of latitude in management actions. This

appeared to be a function of expanding markets for the firm's products (often aided by diversification into new product areas) and the difficulties of market entry for new competitors where the provision of products and services was, in many instances, dependent upon the skills, expertise and innovativeness of highly-qualified employees.

However, as we have already indicated, in some cases product-market pressures were more clearly evident as an influence on the way employees were managed. Some of the computer firms in the study, for example, had experienced not only a decline in growth of the market and increased competition from rival firms, but also technological changes such as increased hardware reliability and software sophistication. They reported a shift to a more customer-orientated approach aimed at selling computer services before and after sales, rather than just selling hardware. For these cases, a need to slim down the company workforce, restructure the skills base in order to shift towards software skills, and to emphasize the importance of the customer focus to employees, were all features of changes in the overall approach to managing employees.

In the case of the electronics companies and some of the R&D laboratories, decline in defence spending, either through the direct receipt of government contracts or indirectly through subcontracting from the contractor, also appeared to be a significant factor. For example, in the case of an independent contract research laboratory, the demand for its services had been in decline over a ten-year period. During this time the market-place had become increasingly competitive as privatized government research establishments and universities entered the market. At the same time the customer base had declined. In the past most work had 'come to' the laboratory on the back of government contracts awarded to other firms. However, government policy was now to encourage contractors to conduct research and development in-house. This meant it was now necessary to actively seek new customers. This set of product-market conditions had a direct effect on the way employees were managed. First, there had been a programme of redundancies resulting in a 30 per cent decline in the workforce over a five-year period. Second, it was emphasized to the predominantly scientific and technical workforce that marketing and selling were now part of their brief, and those with management responsibilities received training in 'prospecting' for new contracts. Third, extremely competitive labour-market conditions and the high cost of living in the South East meant that salaries had to be kept competitive to attract and retain core technical specialists. Fourth, the retirement of the managing director and two assistant directors had meant a new, younger senior management team who introduced new initiatives for improving quality, employee communications and training.

One strong impression from our interviews was that, product markets aside, the most keenly felt external pressure affecting the way employees were managed was in fact exerted by the labour market. During the 1980s the South East of England remained relatively insulated from the effects of unemployment when the economy as a whole was in recession, and from the mid–1980s was at the forefront of the consumer-led boom. White-collar and professional employees were particularly advantaged in these circumstances. Of course, this picture changed considerably at the turn of the decade as recession took hold once again, and this time much more severely in the South. However, most of our interviews were conducted in the late 1980s when a shortage, rather than surplus, of labour was still evident.

Our respondents in the follow-up survey were asked what was the most important personnel or industrial relations issue facing the enterprise. As Table 3.6 shows, our coding of the responses clearly indicates that coping with an active labour market both in recruiting employees and in retaining existing staff was by far the most common difficulty. This is supported by labour turnover figures collected from the establishments which, in the majority of the cases where we were able to acquire such data, were above the national average of 12 per cent for private manufacturing (Millward *et al.*, 1992: 345).

At one establishment, management reported that employee retention had become so problematic that the internal grading structure was becoming distorted by reactive responses to employee threats of resignation:

> putting it bluntly, if you've got the company by the 'short and curlies' in terms of threatening to leave, and you are

Table 3.6 Main personnel/industrial relations issue faced at the follow-up survey establishments

	Establishments citing	
Issue	*No.*	*%*
Recruitment of core staff/skill shortages	12	40
Retaining staff/labour turnover	5	17
Need for new emphasis on training/ retraining	3	10
Management of change	2	7
Other	3	10
None cited	5	17

locked into a terribly important contract that nobody else can do, there have been situations where to sweeten everybody the individual has perhaps been promoted as a means of giving them extra money. A deal is done at the time. (Personnel manager, R&D testing laboratory)

In other cases labour-market shortages had prompted a number of more proactive initiatives. In the case of a medical equipment company, for instance, efforts were being made to look for new pools of labour among women and older job applicants. In another example, one of the Japanese-consumer electronics establishments, recruitment difficulties had prompted a number of initiatives, including an attempt (abandoned because of 'red tape') to set up a crèche, job sharing and training for returners to work and even the purchase of a block of flats to house new employees and offset some of the high living costs associated with the South East.

Conclusion

The main concern of this chapter has been to explore the findings of our follow-up interview survey on management style. While our postal survey findings pointed to a relatively high level of non-unionism in the high-technology sector in the South East, our findings concerning management style do not offer strong support for the view that this was a result of the widespread practice of HRM. In fact, despite this being most commonly associated with high-technology enterprises, our findings point to the relatively limited influence of HRM-type approaches. Instead, we found considerably more variation in how management chose to manage employees, with or without unions. We also sought to explore the importance of product-market factors as an influence on management style. Our findings suggest that, in the main, the approach taken by management was not strongly determined by the product-market pressures. In most cases these were sufficiently weak to allow management a reasonable amount of latitude in how they chose to manage employees. Having said this, it was clear in some cases that changes in the product market had acted as an external impetus to review personnel and industrial relations practices. However, equally important in this respect was the nature of the labour market. In the establishments we studied, shortage of suitably qualified employees and the means to keep them were often as much, if not far more, of a problem than a surfeit of competitors or a shortage of customers.

Notes

1 Having said this, the official definition can also be criticized. For example, it excludes sectors such as biotechnology and, because it is based on characteristics such as the proportion of R&D expenditure against output, the rate of product innovation and the proportion of the workforce employed in administrative, technical and R&D roles, it ignores the actual use made of new technology in the production process itself. In fact, we encountered a number of problems on a case-by-case basis in operationalizing the official definition of 'high technology' when categorizing our establishments in the postal survey. In some instances we were forced to allow our common-sense understandings of the nature of an establishment's activities (gleaned from the questionnaire and/or supporting product information that was supplied) to classify them within the appropriate Minimum List

Headings as specified by the official definition. In recognition of these difficulties, when it came to our case studies, we decided to broaden the definition still further to include settings where advanced technology is used in the firm's production or service provision process (see Beaumont and Harris, 1988).

2 The South East of England was defined in terms of the official geographical region known as ROSELAND ('rest of South East England' excluding Greater London).

3 This was consistent with earlier secondary analysis of the WIRS 1984 data set which found a higher proportion of non-union establishments in the high-technology sector, especially in the South East (using the same definitions as in our survey). However, the 1990 survey suggests that this holds true only if all workplaces (that is, including public sector workplaces) are included. If just private sector workplaces are considered then those in the high-technology sector are no more likely to be non-union than non-high-technology sector workplaces. In fact, in the South East, they are more likely to have recognized unions present. We are grateful to Neil Millward for supplying this information.

4 While our interviews contained questions on overall business strategy, nature of products and the demand for them and so forth, our respondents were primarily personnel specialists. As a result they did not always have, or have to hand, detailed information on this aspect of the enterprise's activities.

4

MANAGING
WITHOUT UNIONS:
CASE STUDIES

_____

A broadly focused 'snapshot' can tell us something about the
general pattern of management approaches in a given industry or
sector. However, for a more realistic understanding of management style, we need to look beyond espoused statements and in
more depth at actual managerial actions at workplace level. In
particular, we need to explore something of the dynamics
through which management approach is articulated and developed over time. Indeed, one point that was evident from our
follow-up interview survey was that the management approaches identified in particular cases were not as static and fixed
as our classificatory schema implied. In the context of dynamic
product-market, labour-market and technological conditions,
many of the approaches were clearly developing or evolving in
particular directions to the extent that, over time, a distinct
evolution, or even change, in style might be judged to have
occurred. It is important to recognize this dynamic, although it is
difficult to capture it adequately through the method of 'one-off'
interviews with one or two key informants in an organization.

The aim of this chapter, therefore, is to explore management
style in non-union enterprises in more depth through an

examination of evidence from our three case-study firms. In particular, we will be concerned with the relationship between overall business policies and the approach taken to managing employees and how this is influenced by product-market pressures. The analysis is taken further in Chapter 6 by exploring the management of change which focuses more explicitly on the dynamics of management style. We begin this chapter with a brief description of the three case-study enterprises.

The case-study companies

Our three case-study companies were: a computer company (COCO); a consumer electronics company (CECO); and a design contractor (DECO) (see Table 4.1).

COCO (UK) was one of 19 wholly-owned international subsidiary operations of a US manufacturer of specialist mainframe computers for complex data analysis. The US company had enjoyed phenomenal growth since its foundation in 1972 and had rapidly expanded into a multinational *Fortune 500* organization. By the end of the 1980s, employment peaked at a worldwide total of over 5200. The UK company had around 240 employees and was responsible for marketing and providing pre- and post-sales technical support. No hardware design or manufacturing was carried out, although some significant software development did take place, and the technical support activities were highly complex.

CECO was a British-owned consumer electronics firm, whose main activity was the manufacture of loudspeakers. The present company had been established following a management buyout in 1984. There were now about 400 employees, mostly unskilled and semi-skilled manual workers involved in assembly operations, but also more highly-qualified technical staff mainly involved in product design and development, and office staff in sales and marketing.

Finally, DECO (UK) was the main one of four British operating divisions of a highly diversified American-owned multinational founded in 1914. The UK operation had been established in 1959 and its principal activity was now the design, on a contract basis,

Table 4.1 The case-study firms

	DECO	CECO	COCO
Activity	Engineering design contractor	Consumer electronics computer	Computer company
Ownership	US	British	US
Employees in Britain	2200*	400	240
World employees	5200	–	30,000
Date founded in Britain	1959	1984†	1978

* DECO was one of four main British divisions of the DECO (UK) holding company. A further 3000 were employed by the other divisions.
† CECO was formed as a result of a management buyout in 1984. Previously the company had been part of a major British consumer electronics group.

of offshore platforms for use in oil and gas exploration and exploitation. The customers were mainly corporate clients operating in the North Sea. The parent company employed over 52,000 employees worldwide, and 2200 of these worked in the main British operating division. The core workforce consisted of design engineers and technicians across a range of engineering disciplines.

Product markets and business strategy

As in the previous chapter we can contrast the product-market circumstances faced by each of these companies in terms of the extent of competitive and customer pressure they faced (see Table 4.2).

For COCO competitive pressures were relatively weak in that the parent company dominated the world market with a 79 per cent share. Market entry into the specialized area in which COCO operated was also very difficult for new competitors. Indeed, such was the specialist nature of COCO's product that when the US company had been founded, industry analysts estimated that the potential customer base was under 100 (in fact 265 COCO computer systems had been installed worldwide by the end of

Table 4.2 The nature of product-market pressures in the three case-study firms

Company	Competitive pressure	Customer pressure
COCO	High market share but downturn in market	A few corporate, public sector and government customers
	Market entry difficult but new Japanese competition	Bespoke products
	Founder's 'spin-off' company creating uncertainty	New customer focus
CECO	*Loudspeakers*:	
	One of few suppliers to major automobile manufacturers	Mainly long production runs to small number of corporate customers
	Growing market share	Long product life cycle determines customer demand
	Consumer electronics:	
	Competitive markets, downturn after consumer boom	Seasonal demand, vulnerable to economic downturns
	Growing market share	Numerous individual consumers
DECO	One of six major firms in the UK, technological leader	Environmental, health and safety regulations, etc.
	Cyclical demand, 'downsizing' and diversification into new sectors.	Small number of large corporate clients with close involvement in projects.

the 1980s, 14 in the UK). The difficult trading conditions of the late 1980s in the computer industry acted as a further barrier to new entrants and two US competitors had left the business in 1989, one a new entrant.

However, the last two years of the 1980s were also difficult ones for COCO. Little or no growth in revenue had occurred and new sources of uncertainty had become apparent. First, COCO computers involved a major investment on the part of the customer, and sales had declined and growth in revenue had flattened out due to cuts in public and corporate expenditure (government clients accounted for 30 per cent of the existing installed systems). Second, in 1989 the founder of the US enterprise decided to leave, taking one-fifth of the assets and several key staff, to create a rival 'spin-off' company to continue development of a new competitor product. Third, COCO's principal current rivals were mainly Japanese and their products were becoming more competitive. This was reflected by the fact that COCO's domination of the Japanese market was less strong than elsewhere. Finally, in 1989 there had been 400 redundancies, the first in the company's history, in the US manufacturing operation. Taken together, these occurrences raised doubts throughout the enterprise about the company's future direction and created a climate in which competitive pressures were perceived by management to be increasing significantly.

Greater pressure was also being felt in the form of a requirement to respond to customer demands for greater connectivity and better post-sales service. In common with most other computer suppliers, COCO's business was increasingly more than just a question of selling hardware to relatively unsophisticated corporate consumers. Products, in particular a range of new 'entry-level' machines, had to be actively marketed and sold as part of an overall service which embraced both pre- and post-sales.

In comparison, CECO was exposed to a far higher level of competitive pressure than COCO. Indeed, the management buyout was a product of such pressures leading the previous owners, a large British-owned electronics group, to withdraw from loudspeaker manufacture in the face of competition from the Far East. However, since the management buyout CECO had enjoyed a period of rapid growth and successful business. Overall, market share had increased to the extent that, in the four years before our study, turnover had quadrupled. The acute competitive pressures which had accompanied the buyout in the early 1980s had thus, relatively speaking, eased by the time of our study.

The period of successful growth had been achieved by a two-pronged business strategy, the key elements of which complemented each other in ways which eased some of the product-market pressures usually faced in the consumer electronics sector. One element of the strategy involved gaining a firm foothold as a supplier of loudspeakers to automobile manufacturers. This had been identified as a new and fast-growing market as factory-fitted in-car entertainment systems were becoming part of the standard specification of vehicles across manufacturers' product ranges. 'Sole-supplier' status had been won from one car manufacturer and additional contracts to supply another four manufacturers had been gained. Subsequently, further contracts and new orders to supply loudspeakers were received from TV and audio firms (which included new British-based Japanese manufacturers).

The second element of the strategy was based on marketing a range of imported consumer electronics products (televisions, telephones, satellite TV equipment, video recorders, microwave ovens and so on). These products were 'rebadged' and then marketed under the CECO brand name. This activity involved a close analysis of market trends which aimed to highlight areas of product-market growth. The main concern was to import products to sell in growing markets. Once market demand stabilized the company ceased imports and stopped marketing the product. For example, as a result of negative publicity concerning safety, growth in the market for microwave ovens had declined. As a result the company had recently decided to cease marketing this product. Attention was then turned to what was at the time seen to be a new growth market, portable telephones, the only other large British supplier being British Telecom.

The seasonal nature of consumer demand and its vulnerability to cyclical movements in the economy are a major source of customer pressure in the consumer electronics industry. For example, most sales of consumer electronics products occur in the pre-Christmas period. In addition, sales are vulnerable to high interest rates, and other factors which depress consumer spending. One benefit of the two-pronged business strategy was

to insulate the company from the worst effects of such pressures. For example, when high interest rates choked off the consumer-led boom in the late 1980s, the company's sales of
loudspeakers to corporate clients remained stable since they
were mainly tied to the six- to seven-year product life cycle of
the automobile industry. Conversely, when the company had
been attempting to broaden its corporate customer base in the
mid–1980s and increase its manufacturing output, buoyant sales
of its imported products had provided an important source of
revenue. In addition, although corporate customers were in a
strong position to demand competitive pricing, reliability and
quality, supplier status also allowed manufacture to be better
planned and organized with longer production runs and a more
efficient utilization of labour. This also served to offset the
seasonal nature of demand, which in many competitor companies normally resulted in short-time working at some points
in the year.

Finally, DECO faced strong competitive and customer pressures. Although, it had a technological lead over its British competitors through the use of computer aided design technology
(see Chapter 6), the market for its design services was highly
cyclical and was tied tightly to the fortunes of the oil and gas
industry. In the 1970s and early 1980s the parent company was
the market leader in offshore contracting. However, in the mid–
1980s the collapse of oil prices resulted in a decline in offshore
contracts. At the same time, the loss of a major lawsuit in the
USA had introduced considerable uncertainty at corporate level.
The US parent had restructured its operations and attempted to
increase co-operation between the operating divisions which,
hitherto, had tended to operate as separate companies. In addition, a programme of redundancies occurred involving the
closure of one of the US operating divisions, with some additional redundancies in Britain. Offshore work had previously
accounted for 90 per cent of workload but, by the time of our
study, diversification into other sectors, such as process plant
design, meant that the proportion had fallen to around 50 per
cent. However, the highly cyclical nature of contract-based business was reflected in the fact that, immediately following this
period of retrenchment, the volume of new offshore contracts in

the pipeline had started to grow once again, and the recruitment of additional staff in the UK was now seen as a priority.

However, it was customer pressures which were the most obvious in DECO's day-to-day operations. The company operated by gaining contracts to design major oil and gas installations, and employees from different discipline departments (structural, piping, heating and ventilation, electrical and instrumentation and so on) were allocated to project teams as required to service the contract. The large investment required on the part of the customer meant that it could exert considerable pressure over the management of the project and the make-up of the project team. This occurred most obviously through the provision of financial incentives and penalties as part of the terms of the contract. These required specified work to be completed on schedule at particular 'milestones'. In addition, the client could exert more subtle pressure by seeking to influence the selection of key personnel on the project and the length of their involvement. An additional source of external pressure was felt in the form of new regulations on matters such as environmental control and, in the wake of such events as the Piper Alfa disaster, increased concern for health and safety.

In sum, on the face of it, the product-market pressures experienced by COCO, and to a lesser extent CECO, were such that management could be expected to have a reasonable degree of latitude in how it chose to manage industrial relations. However, this statement needs to be qualified in both cases. For COCO corporate perceptions of increased product-market pressures had resulted in a new business strategy. One question here is whether this might act as a 'trigger' for changes in the approach to managing employees. Second, in the case of CECO, product-market pressure had become less acute as the business strategy evolved in the wake of the management buyout began to bear fruit. One point here is that it is possible that the room for manœuvre at the point of the buyout on industrial relations matters may have been perceived by management as particularly tight. However, as the enterprise became more successful, management may have become relatively more relaxed about the constraints it faced. Finally, the product-market and customer pressures faced by DECO suggested a particularly strong link would be drawn by management between this and the way employees were managed. With these propositions in mind, we now turn to a discussion of management style in the three case-study enterprises. Again, we will use the concepts of strategic integration and individualism/collectivism employed in the previous chapter to guide our discussion.

COCO: the 'COCO style'

COCO (UK)'s American parent had a well-defined corporate culture and an influential human resources function. Taken together with its typically 'high-tech' origins and subsequent development around a single-product strategy, the management approach to industrial relations and personnel matters in the US bore many of the hallmarks of what is usually regarded as typical of non-union North American-owned computing and electronics companies. In other words, what we have termed 'traditional HRM'. One question, therefore, was how far this approach was 'transplanted' to its British operation and was reflected in high levels of strategic integration between business and personnel/industrial relations policies and practices to the management of employees, combined with a stress on a high degree of individualization of the employment relationship.

In fact, COCO (UK) operated as an autonomous unit as far as most day-to-day operations were concerned. There were some operating policy guidelines from the USA (concerning budgeting, procedures and so on) and contracts for the supply of new computers were signed by the US company. However, in general, high levels of control were not exercised by the US parent on either implementation of business plans or the approach taken to managing employees. Having said this, overall business strategy was defined by the US parent, although senior UK managers were involved in this process.

In terms of the management of employees one clear manifestation of American influence that was apparent was a formal statement of the 'COCO style' found in the UK company 'Employee Handbook' (see Figure 4.1). The importance of the role of this statement was set out by a senior US manager in an internal memo as follows: 'these values guide our behaviours,

'The COCO style'

At COCO, we take what we do very seriously, but we don't take ourselves too seriously.

There is a sense of pride at COCO, professionalism is important. People are treated like and act like professionals. But people are professional without being stuffy.

COCO people trust each other to do their jobs well and with the highest ethical standards. We take each other very seriously.

We have a strong sense of quality – quality in our products and services, of course; but also quality in our working environment, in the people we work with, in the tools that we use to do our work, and in the components we choose to make what we make.

Economy comes from high value, not from low cost. Aesthetics are part of the quality. The effort to create quality extends to the communities in which we work and live as well.

The COCO approach is informal and non-bureaucratic. Verbal communication is key, not memos. 'Call don't write' is the watchword. People are accessible at all levels.

People also have fun working at COCO. There is laughing in the halls, as well as serious discussion. More than anything else, the organisation is personable and approachable, but still dedicated to getting the job done.

With informality, however, there is also a sense of confidence. COCO people feel like they are on the winning side. They feel successful, and they are. It is this sense of confidence that generates the attitude to 'go ahead and try it, we'll make it work'.

COCO people like taking responsibility for what they do and thinking for themselves. At the same time, they are proud to share a single mission – making the world's best computers. Because the individual is key at COCO, there is a real diversity in the view of what COCO really is. In fact, COCO is many things to many people. This consistency comes in providing those diverse people with the opportunity to fulfil themselves and experience achievement.

The creativity, then, that emerges from the company comes from the many ideas of the individuals who are here. And that is the real strength of COCO.

Figure 4.1 The COCO 'Style Statement'
Source: COCO, 'Employee Handbook'

decisions and interactions with all our constituencies – customers, shareholders and communities. They are the values that ensure that COCO is the company we all want it to be.'

How far did this formal espousal of the 'COCO style' influence the attitudes and behaviour of UK managers? In fact, as far as most of the UK managers we interviewed were concerned, the actual style and approach in the UK company was as much, if not more, influenced by the philosophy of the individual who was the managing director. The US-derived style statement and the sentiments it expressed were usually viewed as providing a broad backcloth or general flavour rather than a detailed guide to management practice.

For example, when questioned on the authenticity of the 'COCO style' most managers detected certain resonances with their day-to-day approach but did not view it as a literal account of the way they managed employees. A similar point was made by the UK managing director who commented:

> whether everybody believes every line of it, I frankly doubt very much. But the fact that the company has a style statement I think is important, and when you read it, it gives you an overview of the kind of company it is. Certainly, some of the things that have happened since I have been here lead me to believe that certainly the senior management of this company believe in essentially what is in that statement. Things like 'there will be laughter in the hallways', and 'we behave in a serious way, but we don't take ourselves seriously'. There is every evidence right to the top that the company works in that way.

If not a detailed guide to management practice, the value of the style statement was then certainly not discounted by our managerial interviewees. In the view of the managing director, the 'COCO style' was regarded with 'some reverence by people outside the company'.

The aspect of the style statement that found most resonance in the actual experience of many of the managers interviewed was the objective of retaining a 'small company spirit' through 'organisational developments that promote the formation of small, locally-motivated groups of people'. Indeed, several managers saw COCO as providing an informal and 'fairly ambiguous environment' where there were very few written rules and, where these existed, they were not the sole basis of managerial authority. One comment was that new employees whose previous experience was of working in a more bureaucratic environment often found the COCO approach difficult to cope with.

It was also pointed out that the 'COCO style' could be used as a 'sort of excuse' when things went wrong because there was no set policy or procedure. People had a tendency to say: 'Well, that's the way we do it at COCO.' This was no more so than in relation to personnel policies and practices. Despite the apparently 'people-centred' nature of the style statement, our formal interviews and other contacts with COCO managers and employees made it clear that the company, in Britain at least, was first and foremost 'technologically led'. This meant that issues of personnel policy had to date been given a low priority. One result of this was that, despite the strong human resources function in the US parent, there had never been a specialist personnel manager or personnel specialism within the British company. Instead, personnel matters were one of the responsibilities of the administration manager in the Finance and Administration Department. He, on his own admission, provided only a basic advisory service to line managers on matters such as disciplinary procedures or areas covered by statute (such as maternity leave and sick pay).

In this context, line managers were largely free to make personnel decisions within the broadest of guidelines and, sometimes, if they felt it necessary, outside them. For example, departmental managers enjoyed a wide degree of discretion with regard to matters such as recruitment, training, staff appraisal and pay determination. As a result procedures varied across and within departments, and no standard company-wide policies or formulas were applied, even in key areas such as the setting of pay levels.

It was also the case that there was a predominance of technically qualified managers in senior positions and the tendency for technical achievements to be rewarded by promotion into managerial roles. Previous managing directors were said to have had, to varying degrees, an 'autocratic' approach and little interest in personnel matters. There was also considerable scepticism, if not fear, among some of the middle and more senior UK managers interviewed, concerning the role played by the human resources function in the US. In particular, there was a belief that US line management, with whom UK managers had frequent contact, were constrained in their capacity to deal as they saw fit with people issues. Indeed, it was pointed out that US line managers and even the most senior executives in the USA had similar reservations.[1] The administration manager expressed a commonly held view among middle and senior managers in the UK company, when he commented that in 'fast-moving computer companies' there was not time to develop a 'solid personnel policy'. This of necessity 'dragged behind' because the company had to run 'lean and tight'. Neither would it have been very popular; 'if I go down the corridor and say it ['human resources'] the blokes go 'human resources – what a bunch of tossers and hangers-on!'.

As a result, despite the existence of a coherent statement of the 'COCO style' which seemed to suggest a strong link with the overall business strategy, on closer examination personnel policies and practice in the UK company were revealed to lack formalization and to be poorly integrated. Indeed, in a manner reminiscent of the 'Wild West' approach to managing human resources referred to in Chapter 2, UK line managers appeared free to choose what approach, if any, they were to adopt. As we will see in Chapter 6, in the context of rapid product innovation and related organizational change, the absence of a coherent personnel policy and the means to apply it in practice was to be increasingly highlighted as a source of weakness, especially in the light of an alarming increase in labour turnover and uncompetitive pay levels.

The 'COCO style' statement also placed a great deal of stress on the individual nature of the employment relationship. This was amplified in the 'Employee Handbook', which declared that 'respect for the individual is one of the Company's fundamental beliefs' and that employees should 'feel free to discuss any subject' with their manager and have 'the confidence that he will be sincere in his efforts to provide you with a correct and full answer'. Similarly, the grievance procedure encouraged a 'prompt informal discussion' with the employee's immediate manager if a grievance arose. If this did not resolve the matter it was to be raised with the immediate manager's superiors who were to 'review all aspects . . . and decide on what action, if any, needs to be taken', their decision being 'final'.

In an interesting comment on how this worked in practice, the administration manager pointed out that, in his experience, the procedure rarely reached its final stage. Indeed, he suggested that if things did get that far 'people tended to part company anyway' and that the formal procedure was not particularly relevant in guiding management practice:

> If a secretary has a grievance with her manager she might just as well go because he will probably sack her anyway . . . or agree on terms of departure . . . simply because their relationship has broken down and a grievance procedure will not do any good.

A similar stress on direct individual relationships between managers and employees, but a dislike for rules and procedures, was evident with regard to informing, consulting and communicating with employees. On the one hand a variety of fairly sophisticated communications techniques emanated from the US parent. For example, there was a company newsletter, occasional videos, employee attitude surveys and ballots, and 'Link Up', a question/answer facility for employees to interrogate US managers and directors via the electronic mail system. This procedure had a guaranteed 'comeback' – that is, an answer (or refusal to answer with reasons stated) had to be given within a specified time period. However, on the other hand, as far as UK managers were concerned the key means of communications was through the management chain. This was supplemented by quarterly employee meetings with the UK managing director, who provided information on performance and plans, and *ad hoc* briefings convened by project managers and departmental heads to discuss particular client contracts.

On the central question of why trade unions were absent in the UK company, some managers' attitudes displayed openly hostile attitudes. For example:

> If anybody mentioned the word union here people would shudder. Everything is done on a one-to-one basis like salaries, merit awards, etc.

And when asked what the company's response would be to a union recruitment attempt (reply delivered with some amusement):

> You mean to come and prey on the staff? . . . For a start the majority of the staff are quite mobile so we've got analysts and engineers out on site. We've got a core of people here and they're probably more senior and wouldn't go into a union anyway, I suppose conservative with a small 'c'. I suppose the ones most likely to fall prey are software development who always, to many other departments, appear a bunch of lefties and weirdos.

However, the responses of other managers to this line of questioning suggested that, in general, any anti-union attitudes were a *latent* rather than *active* feature of management policy. Most had not thought deeply about the issue as it simply was not seen as salient.

This had not always been the case. For example, long-serving managers described how a concerted attempt had initially been made to keep unions out when the UK company had been founded in the late 1970s.

> Originally, it came about by design. There was an explicit attempt to create an organization that was not subject to union activities. I remember being asked at my interview: 'Are you going to be a union member at COCO'? . . . My answer was basically no. (Head, Marketing & Sales Support, joined company in 1978)

Overtime unions had simply become a 'non-issue' for the enterprise. Management did not now see any need actively to avoid unionization. This was attributed to the fact that employees saw no need for such representation because of the effectiveness of the managerial approach. As the managing director put it, the organization was run properly, employees were able to express their views, the management style was fairly open, and employees were well paid. As such, 'there shouldn't be any requirement for a trade union. What's the point of a trade union? . . . We're hardly the sort of organization that's treating people badly.'

We will explore the extent to which this sentiment was shared by employees in the following chapter. For the moment, we can note that, as far as the UK company was concerned, the management approach at COCO lacked strategic integration, in particular in terms of the degree of formalization and internal consistency of personnel policies and practices. At the same time, management placed a strong stress on individualism in predominantly informal relations between themselves and employees. Thus, while the US parent appeared to provide an example of 'traditional HRM', the UK company adopted an approach which is more accurately captured by the notion of 'benevolent autocracy'. This is especially so given the high degree of dependence of the company on the high-level skills of its core technical and marketing professionals. Even if not particularly sophisticated or strategic in how it achieved this, management still placed a premium on the recruitment, retention and reward of appropriately skilled and experienced technical employees.

However, one consequence of the corporate perceptions of increased product-market pressure was a parallel recognition that existing personnel policies and practices were not adequate to this task. This was brought home by the fact that, in the year prior to our study, labour turnover had leapt to 30 per cent. It was increasingly being realized that the lack of formalization of policy, and the absence of personnel specialism responsible for standardizing and integrating policy and practice, were a major source of potential weakness which could undermine the new business strategy. We shall see in Chapter 6 how management at COCO responded to this challenge.

Managing a deunionized workforce at CECO

The main feature of the management of employee relations at CECO was that, at the point of the management buyout, all but 50 of a 1000-strong workforce had been made redundant and the trade unions derecognized. A key question for us, therefore, is the nature of the managerial approach that had been developed to cope with the subsequent rapid expansion of the workforce in the absence of unions, particularly the extent to which it had become more strategic and involved a significant shift towards the individualization of the employment relationship.

In fact, personnel policy and procedures at CECO were fragmented and, until just before our study, largely unwritten. Links to overall business policy were tenuous and at best reactive. For instance, although there was an on-site personnel officer who reported to the managing director, she was only responsible for administration, recruitment and welfare matters (estimated at 75–80 per cent of her job). The personnel officer referred to personnel policy at CECO as a 'very grey area' with little 'written down'. In fact, *de facto* responsibility for personnel policy-making had been taken up by the manufacturing manager with whom the personnel officer had a 'dotted line' reporting link. It is also worth noting that, as a result of CECO's growth, a number of small independent hi-fi companies had been purchased and a merger, under the umbrella of a publicly quoted holding company, with another large hi-fi manufacturer had taken place. While matters of engineering and purchasing prompted some standardization, there had been no attempt to standardize personnel policies and procedures across the group as a whole.

However, a recent attempt had been made by the manufacturing manager at CECO to draft a formal written personnel policy. This contained a general statement about employment philosophy 'by the Chief Executive', which amounted to little more than a statement that 'the Directors' wish' was that 'employees would be able to look forward to full and rewarding long term employment with the Company'. The document went on to explain elements of formal policies and procedures on matters such as consultation and grievances. A copy of the full policy had been provided to employee representatives on the staff committee (see below) and it was intended that a short précis would be issued at some point to all employees in the form of a booklet with an endorsement introducing the company by the managing director.

A further insight into management approach can be gleaned from the nature of work and the supervision of labour on the shop-floor. This was driven by line managers' concerns with maintaining the continuity of production and improving output levels. Work was organized and controlled along classic Taylorist lines with a marked degree of occupational segregation between assembly operatives, who were mainly female, and setters and maintenance staff, who were predominantly male. Assembly work was machine-paced and consisted of highly repetitive low-skilled tasks (cycle times ranged from 4.5 to 6 seconds). According to production management, work on the assembly line did not 'require cleverness or a lot of thinking'. This was born out by the low level of training received by line workers (see Chapter 5, Table 5.1).

The monitoring and control of operator performance was also tight and involved both direct supervision and some rudimentary technical surveillance. For instance, once a production job was running, hourly output was recorded on a 'master board' at the end of each assembly line. Along the lines were TV monitors which displayed production targets, the output achieved, and whether production was ahead (in green) or behind (in red) and by how many speakers. These devices were used by the production manager to motivate the staff, by encouraging lines to compete with each other.

The highly gendered division of labour was explained by production management in terms of a belief that males could not cope with assembly-line work, except where it involved the use of a tool, such as when screwing the speaker chassis to the grill. According to the production manager, 'some men would just blow their minds on the assembly line' whereas 'the girls are on autopilot' and had 'a natural skill to do highly repetitive work, at speed, and talk to their colleagues'.

There were rudimentary attempts to 'humanize' the production environment to make the work more 'tolerable'. For example, for what were claimed to be motivational reasons, there was an attempt to keep the same operators on each line in order that friends could sit next to each other. To the same end, the assembly-line work stations were arranged so that operators were seated close enough to enable conversation. Radio music was played in the factory at certain times in the morning and afternoon. There was also recognition that the quality of direct supervision required improvement and that there was a lack of 'people management' skills. One important task facing the company that had been identified, therefore, was to improve the training of its first-line management. In particular, recent changes in the payment system (see below) had added to supervisory responsibilities in periodically assessing staff and allocating them to pay grades.

The character of the management approach was most strikingly revealed, however, by the decision to derecognize the unions. Prior to the 1984 buyout the company had recognized several unions, the principal one being the AUEW. The reason for derecognition appeared to amount to taking advantage of a perceived weakness in the position of trade unions as a result of the Thatcher government's industrial relations reforms and a perception of a moderate tradition in the local labour market. According to the manufacturing manager, employee support for the unions had collapsed in the wake of the redundancy programme before the buyout. After the new company had been formed management and, it was claimed, the remaining employees wanted a 'new start', 'free of past history' and without the trade unions.

The pragmatic stance of management on the question of union recognition was, however, underlined by its reaction to a recent recognition claim. In the year before our study, the EETPU had apparently requested formal recognition on the grounds that it had recruited sufficient members in the plant. Senior management had treated this claim with scepticism, especially as no approach had been made by employees themselves. Nevertheless, if the EETPU persisted in its claim, it was the manufacturing manager's view that the company might have to decide to have an employee ballot. More generally, he suggested that it had to be accepted that demands for union recognition might arise in the future, as memories of how the unions had failed the workforce in the past and how the new management had saved and created new jobs, faded. In particular, new employees may not have the same loyalty to the company and it was possible that in the future demands for union representation might arise. This was a point of some concern to the manufacturing manager, since most of the senior management team had little experience of dealing with unions.[2]

It was also significant that the linchpin of the approach to managing without unions to date had been a company council or committee (known as the 'staff association'). This comprised eleven elected employee members. Its monthly meetings were chaired by the managing director and also attended by the personnel manager.[3] The committee had no formal negotiating role and was intended as a means through which employee views could be gauged, grievances dealt with and information passed to the workforce. However, by the time of our study it was clear that the employee side was far from satisfied with the operation of the committee and was beginning to develop a rather different view of its role. For example, in our interviews with them, employee representatives were prone to question the committee's value. In the view of one employee member, for example, management treated the employee representatives 'like puppets' and tried to use them as 'management mouthpieces'.

In sum, unlike the 'COCO style' which was highly individualized, the CECO approach exhibited many features of collective regulation, most notably in the form of an elected staff committee, but also with regard to pay determination and the treatment of grievances and the management of conflict. At the same time, and more like COCO, the approach to managing employees lacked strategic integration and was more opportunistic and pragmatic. In the case of CECO, personnel and industrial relations matters were strongly subordinated to the requirements of production as seen by line management. As one production manager noted, 'there hasn't been time to do anything but produce speakers, and you cannot afford not to meet the demand'. In such circumstances, the way employees were managed was not dictated by an overall philosophy or style but rather guided by the exigencies that prevailed in particular circumstances (and, it must be said, a set of sexist assumptions concerning the capabilities, attitudes and supervision of female labour). In many ways, the CECO approach was in fact more akin to that of the reactive pragmatism associated with most unionized British firms. Of course, this should not be surprising, given

CECO's earlier recognition of unions. However, it does suggest that CECO managers had failed to develop a clear and consistent alternative to managing with unions and there had certainly not been a fundamental shift in the balance between collectivism and individualism. Indeed, now pressures from the product market were beginning to be felt less keenly, at least compared to when the management buyout had taken place, some managers appeared to have a relatively more relaxed view towards the question of union representation and recognition. We consider employee views on this issue in the next chapter.

DECO: 'looking after the wives'

As in the case of COCO, the management of employees in the UK was not directly influenced by the US parent. At DECO, personnel matters and the personnel function played a marginal role in overall business decision-making and planning and there appeared to be little or no direct influence on personnel policy from the USA. In practice, personnel policy was largely dictated by the managing director and actioned by line management. The personnel specialist's role was mainly one of providing administrative support to line managers.

The US parent had an image as an autocratic and rather traditional employer. However, the 'hire and fire' approach was reported by our British respondents to have 'softened' in recent years, although it was clear that a strong 'machismo' was still evident in the organization's culture. This reflected the physically hard and hostile nature of the environments in which the products being designed were eventually to operate,[4] the particular demands and disciplines imposed by contract-driven project work, and the cyclical nature of demand. In these circumstances it was not surprising that the regulation of the employment relationship was highly individualized and that trade unions were seen as incompatible with the nature of the business in which DECO was engaged.

In fact, the organization of work appeared to reinforce, if not require, a highly individualistic approach to the management of employees. The company was organized on a matrix structure with project management on one axis and engineering disciplines on the other. Individual projects were normally headed by a project manager; project engineers, in charge of engineering and draughting staff drawn from the discipline departments, reporting to the project managers. The composition of the project team in the section varied over the life cycle of the project according to the engineering disciplines required at particular points in time. In some cases the number of staff involved could be quite large – for example, in the pipe-working discipline it was not uncommon to have 100 or more staff allocated to one particular project.

Within this framework there was a premium placed on employee commitment to the project. Getting 'the right person' to 'fit in with the team', in terms of both technical experience and personal qualities, was given a high priority. In addition, there was a need to be able to work under pressure, to be prepared and able to meet deadlines, and to be flexible in order to 'get the job done'. On occasion this meant long hours at short notice, spending periods away from home at the client's site or abroad, and the delay or cancellation of domestic commitments such as family holidays. This was especially the case in the run-up to a project milestone.

Recruitment and allocation of labour to a project was the responsibility of departmental managers in the various engineering disciplines. Discipline managers needed to foster a close one-to-one relationship with their staff and to be able to strike an appropriate balance between the demands of individual projects, the business requirement and the career aspirations and domestic circumstances of individual employees. It was pointed out by our interviewees that, despite the demands it made on employees, the company was a 'people organization' and keen to develop and promote the careers of those individuals prepared to show the appropriate level of commitment. It was not a matter, as one departmental head put it, of 'screwing them to the lowest rate'.

Similarly, senior management was said to be open and responsive: 'it's not uncommon for a draughtsman to talk to a director and mention problems and the next thing that director takes it up'. This encouraged employees to speak up: 'people here are not afraid to make comments and criticisms about how the company works'. Other evidence of the 'soft' people-orientated approach was offered through anecdotes about how project managers often sent flowers to team members' partners at the birth of a baby or if the spouse had been working particularly long hours. On other occasions, senior project staff were permitted by the project manager to take their partners to expensive restaurants paid for out of project funds. In one case, an employee had been asked to cancel a family holiday during a three-month period in which the project team had been working 100-hour weeks. The company then paid for the employee and his family to holiday at Disneyland in the USA. As one interviewee put it, the American style was 'hire and fire' and the British style was 'look after the wives'.

Having said this, management did take a tough approach when employees were seen to be too far out of line. In one memorable incident during an interview with one senior manager, we were witness to a conversation with another manager regarding a disciplinary matter. Our interviewee advised his subordinate, 'Well, hoof him out then' and, turning back to his interviewers, nodded with a grin, 'there's an example of our industrial relations!'.

The highly individualized nature of the employment relationship was demonstrated most clearly in the way pay was determined and by the extensive use of sub-contract labour. Pay was dealt with on a strictly one-to-one basis between employees and their line managers. For example, company policy prohibited discussion between employees over individual rates of pay. Recommendations for pay increases would be made on the basis of subjective judgements of individual performance by immediate supervisors or managers at annual reviews. These were then passed to the relevant discipline manager who, on advice from the personnel department, would make a decision. However, where pay rises were awarded, these still had to be sanctioned by project managers on whose budgets the cost actually fell.

In practice, it appeared that many employees circumvented this formal process and engaged in individual negotiations with project managers. One project manager described such negotiations with a member of his project team as typically being a process of bluff and counter-bluff in the face of employee demands which were usually made in the context of the rates of pay being offered by competitors. As this manager put it, 'these individuals are pretty materialistic. They have allegiance up to a certain point and then its money', and often it was necessary to 'bite your tongue and pay'.

Sub-contract or 'agency' staff were a widespread feature of employment at DECO. Indeed, in one of the departments we looked at, 122 out of 164 staff were on agency contracts. In large part this practice had emerged as a result of a labour-market shortage. However, sub-contracting allowed management greater numerical flexibility in adjusting headcount to suit the overall pattern and volume of workloads on various projects. From the employee viewpoint, working through a sub-contractor allowed most individuals to command substantially higher remuneration, which more than compensated for the loss of job security and other benefits of being a permanent employee.

The cyclical nature of demand, contractual obligations to meet project milestones, strong client pressures, and the need for a high degree of flexibility in the allocation, use and reward of labour, were all seen by the senior managers interviewed as totally incompatible with trade union presence. The view of trade unions was that they would be a handicap to the business and prevent it operating with sufficient speed and fleet of foot to respond to changing market requirements. As such, any suggestion of union organization was seen as a threat and as an unacceptable constraint on the way the business currently operated, and the way in which employees were managed strictly on an individual basis.

For DECO management, therefore, not only the nature of the product market and the particular constraints it imposed, but also the nature of the labour market, underpinned quite directly the organization's non-union status. Unions, rather than being seen simply as an irrelevance, as at COCO, or as something that might pragmatically be avoided, as at CECO, were in this case viewed as fundamentally inconsistent with the achievement of business objectives. In terms of overall management style, as in the other two cases, it does not seem appropriate to characterize the approach as 'human resource management'. In similar fashion to

COCO, the management style was more akin to that of 'benevolent autocracy' where the management prerogative was in DECO's case, also ultimately tempered by the employer's dependence on highly skilled labour which was in short supply on the external labour market.

Conclusion

In this chapter we have outlined the way employees were managed in our three case-study enterprises in the absence of unions. In terms of our analysis in the previous chapter, none of the three case-study firms could be said to have adopted an explicitly HRM-type approach in the sense that there was a high degree of strategic integration between business needs and management style in managing employees. In the case of DECO and CECO, for example, personnel policies were relatively formalized but the personnel function operated in a purely administrative role. In the case of COCO, the situation was more complex. Here personnel policies and practice lacked formalization and were poorly integrated, but this seemed to be in contrast to the US parent's approach which bore many of the hallmarks of 'traditional HRM'. In the case of COCO and DECO, the regulation of the employment relationship was highly individualized. In the case of CECO, however, many of the trappings of a collective approach to managing the employment relationship had been retained following union derecognition. For DECO the internal flexibility required in order to respond to strong product-market imperatives was perceived as underlining the need for unions to be and remain absent. In the case of COCO, external pressures were not perceived as so important in explaining the need for non-union status. In the CECO case, product-market pressures were seen as a key factor in union derecognition, but as these pressures had become less acute it was apparent that management adopted a more pragmatic view of the prospect of future recognition claims. It was noticeable that, in all three cases, the absence of unions was also viewed by management as a reflection of the fact that employees saw no need for them. This is a view which we will now put directly to the test by considering our data on employee attitudes at the three case-study firms.

Notes

1 The UK managing director recounted to us his experience on asking the vice-president of the US parent what he thought of the role of the human resources function. The vice-president replied with some candour: 'Well, if you ask me they're all a bunch of fucking social workers!'
2 The manufacturing manager, in contrast, admitted that he had once been a shop steward and led a strike!
3 In addition, there was also a safety committee which met monthly with three elected employee representatives.
4 Indeed, one aspect of 'surface culture' (Schein, 1992) which was particularly redolent was the nature of the enterprise's headquarters building. Located among other office blocks, the internal decoration, general condition and state of individual offices was more reminiscent of what might be found on the site of a major construction project than at a corporate headquarters!

5

THE EMPLOYEE IN THE NON-UNION ENTERPRISE

So far we have been concerned with management in the non-union enterprise. In this chapter we turn our attention to the employer and the question of why they do not join unions. There are various propositions which might point towards an answer to this question. For example, non-membership may be a function of a withdrawal of support for trade unions consequent on a decline in collective and a rise in individualistic attitudes among employees and society at large (Bassett, 1986; Phelps-Brown, 1990). Alternatively, the lack of an available union to join at a workplace may explain low levels of union membership among employees who are otherwise predisposed to join, reflecting in turn low levels of union recruitment activity outside existing established membership markets (Kelly and Heery, 1989; Willman, 1989; Beaumont and Harris, 1990; Green, 1990; 1992). Finally, management policies of an HRM type might be expected to result in a reduction in employees' demands for union services due to increased commitment to organizational goals and values (Kochan et al., 1986; Dickson et al., 1988; Guest, 1992).

Our main aim in this chapter, therefore, is to examine the reasons for non-membership among employees in our three case-study enterprises. By focusing on the individual employee we are able to examine directly subjective responses to the structural factors which determine union availability in an enterprise (Hartley, 1992: 163–4). We begin by outlining a model of the determinants of the propensity of employees to join trade unions which is consistent with the basic assumptions made by HRM. We then turn to a presentation and discussion of the results of our workforce surveys. As we will see, little support is found for the argument that lack of demand for union services was an attitudinal outcome of managerial policies and practices designed to bring this about. On the other hand, for most employees, lack of an available union to join was not the principal factor either. Rather, the main reason for non-membership appeared to be the instrumental and ideological beliefs concerning unions held by employees themselves.

HRM and individual propensity to join a trade union

In Chapter 2 we saw that a key aspect of HRM theory was a set of personnel policies and practices designed to produce satisfying employment and job conditions, and mechanisms through which communication, consultation and grievance resolution could be achieved. The predicted outcome is an increase in employee commitment to the organization, while demands for union services decrease.

Kochan (1980) provides a model of the 'critical determinants' of the individual's motivation to join a union which contains most of the elements which might be expected to be involved here. A slightly modified version of his model is presented in Figure 5.1. This suggests that, where employees' *satisfaction* with economic aspects of the job (bread-and-butter issues such as wages, benefits, working conditions and the process of pay determination itself) is high, and they have a positive view of the *utility of non-union voice mechanisms* as a means of communication, consultation and grievance resolution, and hold negative *instrumental beliefs* about a union's ability to have an effect on pay and conditions over and above that which an individual might

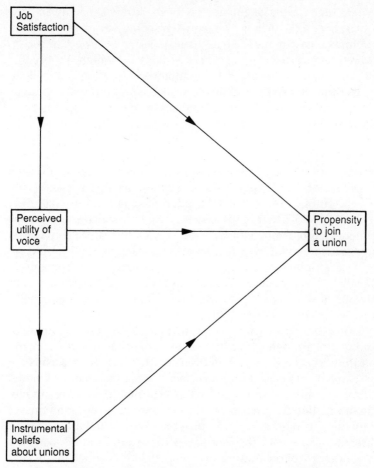

Figure 5.1 Model of critical determinants of propensity to join a union
Source: based on Kochan (1980)

achieve, then their *propensity to unionize* is likely to be low. This would be consistent with the HRM model, provided, of course, such a management approach can be shown to exist, and to have been part of employees' experience of organization membership.

Conversely, if employees experience *dissatisfaction*, this can act as a 'trigger' to union-joining behaviour. This may be reinforced where they have a negative view of the *utility of non-union voice mechanisms* as a means of resolving such grievances. In these circumstances, if individuals have positive *instrumental beliefs*, then their *propensity to join a union* is likely to be high. Where this does not actually result in union membership, then this is likely to be the result of the lack of an available union to join. In other words, the employees' desire for union membership has been frustrated by structural features of the workplace.

We should note that the assumption that job dissatisfaction is the prime motivation for union membership can be criticized because it rests on a crude psychological base, underemphasizes social factors, and implicitly assumes unions are necessary only where employers do not look after their employees (Hartley, 1992: 170, 175–6). It also assumes that dissatisfaction causes union membership. However, it is equally plausible that it is union membership which causes dissatisfaction, for example, by raising employees' awareness of commonly-held grievances. Finally, if dissatisfaction does explain why employees join unions, it does not explain why they remain union members if the sources of dissatisfaction decline or are removed.

However, since our main purpose is to test a model of individual propensity to join a union which broadly fits the assumptions implicit in definitions of HRM, these criticisms are not directly relevant. Moreover, in fairness to Kochan, his model is not one built on crude psychological foundations. For example, dissatisfaction is presented not as the only determinant of individual propensity to unionize but as an 'initial motivator' or 'trigger'. Moreover, the model has the strength of allowing for the influence of other attitudes and behaviours which might lead to union joining and which themselves reflect social influences both within and outside the workplace (Hartley, 1992: 170). In addition, for our concerns, the question of causality is not particularly relevant since this is presumably most problematic where employees are being asked, after the event, about the motivation which initially led them to join, making it difficult to disentangle whether dissatisfaction is a cause or effect of this behaviour. Similarly, we are not concerned with why employees remain union members and neither is Kochan's model intended to explain this.

Propensity to unionize among COCO, CECO and DECO employees

Our employee sample is constituted by four surveys conducted in the three case-study enterprises. The DECO workforce was comprised of qualified professional engineers responsible for basic conceptual design, and technician-level engineers responsible for detail design and drafting tasks. It was the latter which were the focus for our survey.[1] At CECO, the bulk of the manual workforce was located mainly on the loudspeaker production lines, but also included maintenance workers, setters and operatives from other production areas. In addition, a much smaller group of non-manual employees were concerned with research and development, sales and marketing and administrative support. Separate surveys were conducted of both the manual and non-manual workforces. Finally, at COCO, the workforce was mainly comprised of highly qualified computer professionals and technicians engaged in sales, marketing and technical support activities. The bulk of this workforce (excluding the mobile sales force and technical support staff located at customer sites) were the focus of our survey.

As the foregoing suggests, the characteristics of the surveyed workforces differed in a number of significant respects (see Table 5.1). For example, of the four, the CECO manual workforce was predominantly female and young, the lowest educated and paid, the least extensively trained, and had the shortest employment experience. In contrast, the COCO computer technicians were the most highly educated, the best paid, and most extensively trained. The DECO technicians and CECO non-manual staff mainly exhibited characteristics between these two extremes, although the former were all male and were the workforce with the most employment experience, and the latter were the most likely to have experienced being made redundant. The one common characteristic across the four samples was a very low level of union membership (see Table 5.1). Overall, out of the total sample of 215 respondents only 5 per cent were currently union members, although 30 per cent had been union members in the past. The central question of this chapter, therefore, concerned the vast majority of the employees who responded to our surveys.

Table 5.1 Main characteristics of the workforce survey samples (per cent)

	DECO Technicians	CECO		COCO Computer staff
		Manuals	Non-manuals	
Current union member	0	4	3	2
Previously union member	25	25	41	29
Female	0	81	46	12
Age:				
16–29	23	60	32	46
30–39	34	14	38	34
40+	43	26	30	20
Highest educational qualifications:				
None	7	56	30	0
CSE/O level/HNC/ONC/ C&G	84	44	67	32
Degree or higher	9	0	3	68
Net pay per annum:				
<5K	NA	57	0	0
5K to 6K	NA	43	62	0
10K to 21K	NA	0	32	76
21K+	NA	0	24	24
On-the-job training:				
None in last 12 mths	3	41	47	5
1 day in last 12 mths	54	25	17	6
2+ days in last 12 mths	43	44	36	89
Off-the-job training:				
None in last 12 mths	3	83	42	25
1 day in last 12 mths	79	12	18	4
2+ days in last 12 mths	18	5	40	71
Years in full-time employment:				
1–5	16	41	11	33
6–10	4	18	16	23
11–20	32	18	35	32
21+	48	23	38	12
Number of previous employers:				
0–2	32	37	24	46
3–5	32	37	49	45
6+	36	27	27	9
Years with company:				
0–2	11	60	43	45
3–5	9	21	16	34
6–19	34	18	35	21
20+	46	1	6	0
Made redundant in past	30	29	41	6

Table 5.2 Job satisfaction*

Item	DECO	CECO		COCO	All
		Manual	Non-manual		
Pay	61 (91)	21 (66)	19 (62)	25 (77)	30 (73)
Benefits	38 (51)	38 (56)	41 (38)	84 (45)	61 (49)
Skill use	86 (77)	41 (33)	81 (54)	86 (83)	71 (61)
Training	56 (33)	22 (39)	39 (22)	73 (50)	47 (38)
Job security	68 (58)	64 (61)	75 (60)	72 (60)	69 (60)
Supervision	68 (63)	54 (38)	65 (41)	72 (70)	64 (53)
Overall job satisfaction	65	24	43	50	43

* Figures are percentages of staff satisfied with each item (percentages of staff prepared to quit if dissatisfied given in parentheses).

Job satisfaction

The first point we wished to establish was the extent to which employees in the three workforces could be judged to be satisfied or dissatisfied with their jobs in relation to bread-and-butter issues such as pay and conditions.[2] As Table 5.2 shows, the level of job satisfaction was highest in the cases of DECO, COCO and CECO non-manual workforces, with 65, 50 and 43 per cent respectively expressing overall satisfaction in terms of a range of job characteristics such as pay, benefits and so on. The least satisfied were the CECO manuals, where under a quarter could be judged to be satisfied overall. One obvious point to note here is that in only one case, the DECO technicians, were a clear majority of employees satisfied with their job overall.

When looked at in relation to specific issues, some important variations become apparent, especially with regard to pay. Only in the case of the DECO technicians were a majority of employees satisfied with this aspect of the job. In the case of the other three workforces, at least three-quarters of employees were not satisfied with their pay. The low level of satisfaction on this item recorded by the COCO computer staff is particularly striking, since on all other items, except training, the majority were satisfied. Pay, therefore, was a particular bone of contention for COCO employees.

In order to assess the importance attached to dissatisfaction over a particular item, respondents were also asked if they would be prepared to quit if they were dissatisfied with that particular aspect of their job. As one would expect, responses varied according to the particular item concerned, with pay being the only one on which a majority of respondents from all four workforces would be prepared to quit. In the case of the DECO technicians, the group with highest current satisfaction with this aspect of their job, virtually all said they would quit if they became dissatisfied.

In sum, the overall level of job satisfaction among the four workforces was, with the exception of the DECO technicians, low. This was clearly the case overall for CECO manual and non-manual employees, and for COCO employees on the specific item of pay. Therefore, sufficient grievance might be said to exist among at least three of the workforces for the level of dissatisfaction with the job to become a 'trigger' to union-joining behaviour. For reasons already discussed, job dissatisfaction alone cannot be expected to result in wanting to join a union. Indeed, that a significant proportion of employees were prepared to quit if they became dissatisfied over an item such as pay, should also alert us to the fact that the option to 'exit' from the organization may be more appealing to a dissatisfied individual than staying and seeking to join a union.

Non-union voice mechanisms

Of course, quitting is not the only option available to employees when they are dissatisfied with one or more aspects of their job. Another option is to seek to bring grievances to management's attention in order to have them resolved. Grievance handling is one function of what we have referred to as non-union voice mechanisms. Two other elements of management approach can also be regarded as important here: first, the disclosure of information on matters such as business performance; and second, consultation with employees over changes that directly concern their job. Three items in our questionnaire covered these aspects of non-union voice mechanisms, inviting respondents to indicate how far they saw these in a positive or negative light. For example, with regard to grievances, respondents were asked whether or not it would be worthwhile complaining to management if a grievance arose. The answers to this and the two other questions were ranked to give a scale of the perception of the utility of the non-union voice mechanisms.

As we saw in the previous chapter, management in the case-study enterprises provided various means by which information disclosure, communication and consultation could take place, although it will be recalled that in none of the cases were the non-union voice mechanisms notable for their sophistication. Both COCO and DECO relied largely upon the management chain as the main mechanism through which employee grievances could be articulated and any conflict managed. In the case of CECO, a staff committee with elected employee representatives had been created following the derecognition of unions.

Our findings on the 'perceived utility' of these non-union voice mechanisms are summarized in Table 5.3. Overall, just over half of the surveyed employees viewed the voice mechanism in their enterprise positively. This was most marked for the DECO technicians and COCO employees, well over two-thirds in each case giving positive responses. In the case of CECO non-manuals, slightly over half responded positively. However, nearly two-thirds of CECO manual employees responded negatively. The CECO manual and non-manual workforces were also asked about the utility of the elected staff committee. However, both in terms of grievance handling and as a means of information provision (a question concerning consultation was not asked), a clear majority of both manual and non-manual employees answered in negative terms.

As far as the DECO and COCO employees were concerned, our findings would seem to suggest that any 'trigger' to union joining given by dissatisfaction with the job was *not* being reinforced by negative views on information disclosure, consultation or grievance handling. However, for the CECO manuals and non-manuals, there was clearly a possibility that this was the case. For the CECO manuals, in particular, relatively high levels of overall dissatisfaction were combined with negative views of the voice mechanism. This also seemed to be so for the CECO

Table 5.3 Perceived utility of non-union voice mechanisms
(per cent)

	DECO	CECO		COCO	All
		Manual	Non-manual		

(a) Perception of the utility of management grievance handling,
information provision and consultation.

Positive perception	73	35	53	71	57
Negative perception	27	65	47	29	43

(b) Perception of the utility of the staff committee in information
provision (CECO only)

Positive perception	–	38	40	–	39
Negative perception	–	62	60	–	61

non-manuals, especially when their views on the utility of the
staff committee were considered.

Instrumental support for trade unions

The third point we sought to establish was the extent to which
employees were prepared to judge trade union representation as
a potential instrumental benefit to them. In order to assess this
we asked about attitudes towards a union negotiating pay in the
context of questions regarding other possible methods of pay
determination such as making a collective approach without a
union but with fellow employees, negotiating with management
individually, or letting management alone decide. Overall, just
over a quarter of employees in the four workforces 'agreed' or
'strongly agreed' (the rest either 'disagreed' or 'strongly disagreed') with the proposition that a union should negotiate their
pay; just over half with the proposition that a collective approach
with other employees should be made; just over two-thirds with
the view that they should put their own case; and just over half
that pay-setting should be left to management (see Table 5.4).
As one would expect, the four workforces differed in the

Table 5.4 Preference for different modes of pay determination (per cent)

	DECO	CECO		COCO	All
		Manual	Non-manual		
Trade union to negotiate:					
Agree/strongly agree	5	68	16	8	27
Disagree/strongly disagree	95	32	84	92	73
Joint approach with other employees:					
Agree/strongly agree	32	88	36	35	52
Disagree/strongly disagree	68	12	64	65	48
Put own case:					
Agree/strongly agree	82	52	67	75	68
Disagree/strongly disagree	18	48	33	25	32
Management to determine:					
Agree/strongly agree	50	44	53	62	52
Disagree/strongly disagree	50	56	47	38	48

support they showed for the various methods of pay determination. The vast majority of CECO manuals supported having a trade union to negotiate pay and making a collective approach with other employees. Conversely, the idea of making an individual approach or leaving pay-setting to management was much less strongly supported. In contrast, the majority of CECO non-manuals firmly rejected both the idea of a trade union to negotiate pay on their behalf and a collective approach with other workers. In the case of the DECO technicians and the COCO computer staff, opposition to the idea of a trade union to negotiate pay was overwhelming. The idea of a collective approach with other employees was also weakly supported by CECO non-manuals, DECO technicians and COCO computer staff. The vast majority gave their support to individuals making their own case to management. These three workforces were less likely, however, to support the idea of management alone setting pay, although over three-fifths of COCO employees supported this proposition.

In sum, our findings here suggest that, in comparison to dealing with management on an individual basis or leaving matters entirely to them, the DECO technicians, CECO non-manuals and COCO computer staff all saw little advantage in having their pay determined by a union or through a collective approach with colleagues. Conversely, CECO manuals saw particular advantage in a collective approach, either with other workers, or through a union.

Propensity to join a union

The final step in this part of our discussion is to see how far overall job satisfaction, perceptions of the voice mechanism and instrumental beliefs about unions were reflected in a propensity to join a union. An indication of each individual's propensity to join a union was established through a question which asked why, if they were not union members, this was so. Initially respondents were provided with three possible reasons and asked to indicate which was most appropriate to them. The three reasons were: they were not a union member because they were against unions in principle; they did not join because of management opposition; or they did not join because there was no union available to join. The latter two responses were subsequently recoded as showing a 'propensity to join', and the first as 'no propensity to join' – in the sense that, even if a union were available and there was no perceived management opposition, they would still *not* join.

Overall, half of the employees showed 'no propensity to join a union' (see Table 5.5). This was most pronounced among the CECO non-manuals (69 per cent), followed by the DECO technicians (62 per cent) and the COCO computer staff (58 per cent). However, a propensity to join was found among 68 per cent of the CECO manual employees.

Table 5.5   Propensity to join a union
(per cent)

	DECO	CECO		COCO	All
		Manual	Non-manual		
No propensity to join	62	26	69	58	50
Propensity to join	36	68	31	38	46
Uncoded answer	2	6	0	4	4

Placed in the context of our findings concerning job satisfaction, perception of non-union voice mechanisms and instrumental beliefs about unions, these results appear to give prima facie support for our adaptation of Kochan's model. For example, a propensity to join a union was found in the manual workforce at CECO, which also exhibited low levels of job satisfaction, a negative perception of the utility of the non-union voice mechanism (including the elected staff committee), and a high instrumental support for collective as opposed to individual pay determination. Similarly, no propensity to join a union was evident among the DECO technicians and COCO computer staff. In both cases, as the model predicts, this was accompanied by relatively high levels of job satisfaction (although this was not the case for COCO employees on the specific item of pay), a high perceived utility of the non-union voice mechanism, and a more negative view of union and collective involvement in negotiating pay.

Indeed, the propensity to join a union exhibited by the manual workforce at CECO is consistent with the picture of industrial relations at the company that emerged in the previous chapter. As we saw, there was evidence of an emerging collectivization of the workforce, both in terms of the behaviour of workers' representatives on the staff committee, and in the way workers themselves were beginning to articulate their grievances, especially with regard to the issue of working conditions. The propensity to join a union is also noteworthy because, although engaged in low-skilled manual assembly work, conventional wisdom suggests that a young and predominantly female work-force should not be particularly predisposed to union member-ship.

Part of the explanation for this propensity to unionize might have been that the company had a previous history of union organization and that a significant rump of current or ex-union members remained. However, as we noted earlier, only a tiny proportion were still current union members. Moreover, the majority of shop-floor employees were made redundant at the point of the management buyout and derecognition in 1984. As a result, very few of the current manual workforce had been employed by the company when unions were recognized. Indeed, three-fifths of the employees in our survey had been with CECO for two years or under and only 6 per cent with the company prior to derecognition.

Put alongside these findings, the absence of a propensity to join on the part of most CECO non-manuals is also worthy of further comment. Like their manual counterparts, the CECO non-manuals exhibited a relatively high level of overall job dissatisfaction. Unlike their manual colleagues, however, dis-satisfaction with the job did not seem to 'trigger' union-joining behaviour, or at least an attitudinal response which showed a high propensity to join a union. This might have been explained if this group had seen the non-union voice mechanism in a positive light – in other words, they felt that job-related griev-ances could be resolved by complaining to management and that information provision and consultation were adequate. How-ever, like the manual workforce, in reality they viewed the utility of the staff committee – the core of the non-union voice mechanism – negatively. Overall, therefore, grievances and the like did not appear to be perceived as being dealt with adequately by management.

However, unlike the manual staff at CECO, the non-manuals did not support the idea that collective approaches to pay determination would be more beneficial than individual methods. Rather, they appeared to view 'putting up' with job dissatisfaction, in the context of a management unwilling or unable to resolve their grievances, as a more viable behaviour than joining a union. Given this, it was surprising that when asked if they would quit if dissatisfied over a particular aspect of their job, on three out of the four items including pay, CECO non-manuals were the least likely of the four workforces to say that they would leave voluntarily (see Table 5.2), although over half said it would be 'very easy' or 'easy' to find another job. For these employees neither management nor union provided an effective means of redress, and, even in an active labour market, staying put and 'lumping it' rather than 'voting with their feet' was apparently the preferred option.

A point to note here is that over two-fifths of the CECO non-manuals had previously been union members, far more than in the other three workforces. It was also the case that two-fifths of the non-manual respondents had been with CECO prior to the buyout, so they might have had strong memories of the trade unions' inability to prevent redundancies. One proposition could therefore be that previous membership and employment experiences were reinforcing negative instrumental views of unions as an effective means of resolving job-related grievances. The CECO non-manual sample size was too small to allow us to test this. We therefore attempted to establish to what extent the 30 per cent of our *overall* sample of employees with previous union membership experience were more likely to have no propensity to join than the 70 per cent of employees who had never been union members. However, while statistically significant, our results were inconclusive. Nevertheless, it is worth recording this point as worthy of further research since a study of non-union employees working for IBM also noted previous experience of working in a unionized environment as one factor explaining current non-union membership (see Dickson *et al.*, 1988).

The relative effect of factors determining propensity to join a union

The above analysis tells us nothing about the *relative* contribution of the three independent variables (*job satisfaction, perceived utility of non-union voice mechanisms* and *instrumental beliefs*) on the dependent variable *propensity to join a union*. The model clearly gives primacy to high levels of job dissatisfaction as a necessary 'trigger', though not itself a sufficient determinant, of union-joining

Table 5.6 Logit model, no propensity to join a union: version 1

Parameter	Lambda coefficient	Odds	Odds ratios	Significance
Constant	−0.5112	0.360		0.001
Satisfaction:				
satisfied	−0.0073	0.986	1.064	0.960
dissatisfied with pay	0.0453	1.095	1.181	0.741
dissatisfied	−0.0379	0.927	1	0.797
Perception of voice mechanism:				
positive	0.2363	1.604	2.575	0.019
negative	−0.2363	0.623	1	
Instrumental view of unions:				
negative	0.8625	5.223	27.35	<0.001
positive	−0.8625	0.191	1	

Model is [P] [PS] [PV] [PI], where P = propensity to join a union; S = satisfaction; V = perception of voice mechanism utility; and I = views on union instrumentality.

Model statistics: $L^2 = 5.24$, df = 7, $p = 0.63$.

behaviour. Further light was thrown on our findings in this respect through a log-linear analysis. This allowed us to assess the relative contribution of the three independent variables.

The results of this analysis (see Table 5.6) revealed that *instrumental beliefs* about unions had the strongest effect and that the effect of the other variables was far weaker. If employees had *negative* views of unions in instrumental terms, this raised the odds that they would have *no* propensity to join by a factor of 5.2. *Perception of the utility of the voice mechanism* was the next most important variable, although if employees had a *positive* view of the voice mechanism in their enterprise, this only raised the odds of their having *no* propensity to unionize by a factor of 1.6. Contrary to expectation, the *extent of job satisfaction*, whether overall or on the specific item of pay, appeared to have little or no effect on propensity to join a union.

Further, if respondents had negative views of the instrumental value of unions the odds were over 27 times as great that they would *not* want to join a union as compared to those who had positive views. If respondents had positive views of the utility of management voice mechanisms the odds were nearly 2.6 times as great that they would *not* want to join unions as compared to those who had negative views. If individuals had a high level of overall job dissatisfaction the odds on their having a propensity to join a union or not were more or less even. This was also the case when dissatisfaction with regard to pay was considered.

On the basis of this analysis, as far as the question of the withdrawal of employee support versus union availability is concerned, it appears that in the case of the CECO manual workforce unavailability was the key reason for non-union membership. If a union were to become available, the majority of these employees would, on the basis of our attitude survey, join. In the case of the other three workforces, it appeared that union availability would make no difference to the majority who held negative instrumental views of unions. Having said this, it should be noted that at least 30 per cent of the DECO technicians, CECO non-manuals and COCO computer staff exhibited a propensity to join a union, at least in the sense that their reasons for non-membership were not based on principled opposition.

These findings do not appear to offer much support for the notion that the practice of HRM was responsible for the propensity of employees to join a union. Neither job satisfaction nor non-union voice mechanisms appeared a strong influence, whereas these are seen by theories of HRM as a key element in reducing employee demands for union services. Of course, given our earlier observations regarding management style in the three case-study firms, this should not come as any surprise.

Organizational commitment

We were able to explore further the factors determining propensity to join a union by examining the extent to which the employees in the four workforces exhibited high levels of commitment to the organization. Following HRM theory, it might be anticipated that knowledge of the degree of commitment of an individual employee to the values and goals of the enterprise should, in so far as union membership challenges the interests of the organization, be a factor predicting propensity to join a union (Guest, 1992: 120). Therefore, it might have been that, notwithstanding our findings on job satisfaction and non-union voice mechanisms, those employees with no propensity to unionize exhibited high levels of organizational commitment. If so, this would at least be consistent with, if not entirely explained by, an HRM model.

A considerable amount of attention has been devoted to the question of defining and measuring organizational commitment (see, for recent discussions, Lincoln and Kalleberg, 1990; Dillon and Flood, 1992; Guest, 1992; Coopey and Hartley, 1993). This is not the place to review this extensive literature, suffice it to say that in our survey we were concerned with the extent of 'moral' commitment exhibited by employees – that is, the extent to which they subscribed to a unitary view of the organization, and accepted organizational goals and values as their own (Guest and Dewe, 1991: 77, following Etzioni, 1961). Arguably, it is commitment in this sense that HRM in the non-union firm would be intended to achieve.

According to Mowday et al. (1982) organizational commitment so defined has the following characteristics: a willingness to work hard on behalf of the organization; a desire to maintain membership of the organization; and acceptance of the goals and values of the organization. Our questioning on organizational commitment was based on items selected to reflect these three attitudinal characteristics from Mowday et al.'s (1982) widely used organizational commitment scale.

Our findings can be summarized as follows (see Table 5.7). First, the vast majority of employees in all four of the surveyed workforces appeared to be highly committed to working hard for the organization, beyond what was expected, in order to help it succeed. As such, this did not appear a particularly useful way to discriminate between different levels of commitment, and further statistical analysis suggested that we should drop this item as a measure of organizational commitment.[3]

Second, there were marked variations between the four workforces in the extent to which they indicated a desire to remain organizational members. This desire was tested through a number of questions, namely whether the employee would leave

Table 5.7   Organizational commitment (percentage 'agreeing' or 'strongly agreeing' with item statement)

Item	DECO	CECO		COCO
		Manual	Non-manual	
'I am willing to put in a great deal of effort beyond that normally expected to help this company succeed'	91	75	95	85
'I would accept almost any type of job assignment in order to keep working for this company'	20	47	21	11
'I could just as well be working for another company as long as the type of work was similar'	42	61	52	46
'I could just as well be working for another company as long as the pay was similar'	49	61	54	32
'I would leave this company and move to another company for a slight increase in pay'	23	56	33	23
'I find my values and this company's values are very similar'	54	35	56	65

the company for a slight increase in pay, leave for another job if the pay were the same, leave for another job if the work were the same, or was willing to accept any job in order to remain with the company.

The employee's willingness to leave the company for a *slight increase* in pay, is viewed by Lincoln and Kallenberg (1990) as a key indicator of commitment in the Mowday *et al.* scale. If we take answers to this item as an overall guide then, in the case of DECO and COCO employees, over three-quarters responded negatively, saying they would not leave the company. In the case of CECO non-manuals, over two-thirds also responded in the negative. The exception was the CECO manual workforce, a slight majority of whom said that they would leave the company for a job that paid slightly better. The answer to the other questions which sought to gauge willingness to remain an organizational member broadly followed this pattern, with the CECO manuals showing lower levels of organizational commitment than the other three workforces.[4]

Third, in terms of the extent to which employees identified with the values and goals of the organization, the most highly committed workforce was that at COCO, with nearly two-thirds agreeing with the proposition. In the case of CECO non-manuals and DECO employees, a slight majority agreed with the proposition. However, nearly two-thirds of CECO manuals disagreed. If, as Guest and Dewe (1991) argue, identification with company goals and values is the core of organizational commitment, then our results on this item should be taken as the strongest indicator of organizational commitment among the surveyed workforces.[5]

Organizational commitment and propensity to join a union

We can now consider the relationship between organizational commitment and propensity to join a union. Our basic findings showed that both willingness to remain an organizational member and identification with the organization appeared to have a relationship with propensity to unionize. That is, for the overall sample, the less willing employees were to remain a member of the organization, the more likely they were to show a propensity to unionize. Conversely, the more employees wanted to remain an organizational member, the more likely it was that they exhibited no propensity to join a union. Similarly, those employees who indicated a high commitment to the values and goals of the enterprise were less likely to exhibit a propensity to unionize than those who indicated a low identification.

In order to explore this further we included these two variables in our logit modelling exercise. At the same time we left out our 'job satisfaction' variable which we have already established had little or no effect, relative to perceptions of the voice mechanism and instrumental views of unions, on the dependent variable, propensity to join. We also included another variable which we suspected might have some influence, namely respondents' 'ideological' predisposition towards unions as indicated by responses to two questions: whether they thought unions had too much power and whether they felt most people need an organization such as a trade union to protect their interests.

In fact, ideological beliefs about unions, be they positive or negative, are seen by the Kochan model as a weak source of motivation to join a union. Employees with ideological objections to unions are assumed to allow these to be outweighed by strong instrumental motivations and vice versa. However, the basic findings from our survey suggested a stronger relationship with propensity to unionize. For example, the workforce with the highest proportion of employees with a propensity to join, the CECO manuals, was also much more favourably disposed towards unions in ideological terms than the majority of their counterparts in the three other workforces, who were also more likely to have no propensity to unionize.

As it turned out, neither of the organizational commitment variables had a statistically significant influence on propensity to join a union in this exercise and were dropped from the statistical model at an early stage. Similarly, although statistically significant, the effect of respondents' perceptions of the voice mechanism was slight enough for this also to be left out of the model. This meant that how respondents judged unions in instrumental terms as a method of pay determination was still the main factor determining their propensity to unionize (see Table 5.8). Negative instrumental views of unions raised the odds of having no propensity to join by a factor of just over 3.2. Ideological beliefs about unions also had a statistically significant but weaker influence on propensity to join. Disagreement with the proposition that most people need trade unions to represent them and agreement with the proposition that trade unions are too strong, raised the odds of having no propensity to unionize by a factor of just over 2. Further, the odds of an employee with negative instrumental beliefs about trade unions having no propensity to join, were 10.5 times as great compared to the employee who had positive beliefs. Where employees felt that most people did not need a trade union, or felt unions were too strong, the odds were

113

Table 5.8 Logit model, no propensity to join a union: version 2

Parameter	Lambda coefficient	Odds	Odds ratios	Significance
Constant	−0.3688	0.478		0.017
Instrumental view of unions:				
positive	−0.5865	0.309	1	<0.001
negative	0.5865	3.232	10.5	
People need trade unions:				
agree	−0.3936	0.455	1	<0.001
disagree	0.3936	2.197	4.83	
Unions are too strong:				
disagree	−0.3911	0.457	1	<0.001
agree	0.3911	2.186	4.78	

Model is [P] [PI] [PN] [PS], where P = propensity to join a union; I = views on union instrumentality; N = views on proposition that most people need unions; and S = views on proposition that unions are too strong.

Model statistics: $L^2 = 5.758$, df = 4, $p = 0.218$.

When perceptions of voice mechanism utility were added to this model, all variables were statistically significant, but the resulting model had 'too strong' a fit: $L^2 = 5.87$, $p = 0.856$.

nearly five times as great that they would *not* want to join unions as compared to those who held the opposite views.

In sum, the results of our questioning on organizational commitment and further statistical modelling of the factors determining propensity to join a union appear to strengthen our earlier conclusions. That is, our analysis suggests that the fact that the majority of CECO non-manuals, the DECO technicians and COCO computer staff had no propensity to unionize, was *not* the result of the practice of a management style which reduced employee demands for union services. Rather, this was primarily the result of the negative instrumental value these employees saw in union membership, and, to a lesser extent, ideological beliefs that were antagonistic towards trade unions. Conversely, the fact that the majority of the CECO manual workforce exhibited a propensity to unionize was a function of instrumental and ideological beliefs more favourable to trade unions.

While we did not set out to collect systematic qualitative evidence of views regarding trade unions, it is worth concluding our discussion in this chapter with comments from the employees' themselves. These illustrate many of the attitudes and perceptions underlying our quantitative analysis. For example, the following comments indicate how union membership was judged by COCO employees as irrelevant in an active labour market and in the context of relatively favourable working conditions and terms of employment:

> The computer industry is so competitive that if you don't like it you can go out and get five job offers if you are any good at all. So, I mean, my personal opinion is that we're better off without any unions.

> The company has always challenged me and is a fun company with a very open management style. I have never considered the need for a trades union.

> In the highly mobile industry of computing jobs the value of unions is limited as most people vote with their feet. However, I agree in principle with the trade union movement. (Former union member)

Finally, comments from the CECO manual employees clearly illustrated a high level of dissatisfaction with aspects of their work and relations with management, although we would again stress that our statistical analysis does not suggest that such views were a strong determinant of propensity to join a union:

> I do not intend staying at CECO any longer than I have to. As for the work and the hours we do the pay is useless, especially now that we have poll tax to pay plus clothe the kids . . . all in all the company stinks.

> CECO is Victorian in its attitudes towards employees.

> We are never consulted by management about any changes that involve us. If we point out faults in their way of running things we are ignored and expected to cope, instead of listening to us who have to do the job day after day. They think they know best.

Communication between management and workers is virtually nil.

If CECO . . . respected employees a bit more . . . and treated people as people instead of machines, they might find we would co-operate a lot more.

Conclusion

In this chapter we have sought to establish why individual employees in three non-union enterprises were not union members. The question was one that concerned the vast majority of respondents in four workforce surveys, 95 per cent of whom were not union members. The evidence we have presented suggests that lack of union availability explained this very low level of union membership in only one of our surveyed workforces, the CECO manual workers. The majority of these employees exhibited a propensity to join which, it might be anticipated, was clearly being frustrated by union absence. In this instance union presence might well result in favourable employee attitudes being converted into union-joining behaviour, a point which we will explore further in the next chapter.

In the case of the non-manuals at CECO, the DECO technicians and the COCO computer staff, lack of an available union to join did not appear to explain non-membership for the vast majority of employees. In these cases union presence would apparently have made no difference and most employees might be expected not to join even if a union became available. Having said this, a significant minority did exhibit a propensity to unionize. These findings are consistent with those presented earlier concerning management style. The absence of a propensity to unionize among employees did not appear to be an attitudinal outcome associated with high levels of organizational commitment as envisaged by models of HRM. Rather, non-membership appeared to have more to do with an individual's instrumental and ideological beliefs about unions than the sophistication of the approach adopted by management towards industrial relations.

Notes

1 Because of the terms of access, our sample was restricted to technicians who had undertaken CAD training. These accounted for about three-quarters of full-time engineering staff. This feature of the sample should be borne in mind when considering their views on questions such as technical change (see Chapter 6) since those who had not been retrained were largely individuals who were said by management to be resistant to the new technology. DECO also employed a high proportion of sub-contract staff (see Chapter 4), and these were excluded from the survey.

2 Respondents were asked how important particular job characteristics were to them and how far their present job exhibited these. These responses were then used to classify respondents on the scale of overall satisfaction/dissatisfaction with their present job. The more their current job exhibited characteristics they had deemed important to them in a job, the more respondents were judged to be satisfied with their job.

3 The fact that the CECO manual workforce was otherwise not particularly highly committed to the organization, as indicated by our other measures, suggests that the findings on willingness to work hard for the organization in their case need to be interpreted slightly differently. Perhaps most employees are, in principle, prepared to work hard for their employer. However, such commitment may be undermined where its existence goes unrecognized or unrewarded. It is noteworthy, for example, that the CECO manuals were the least likely to say that their supervisors recognized good performance.

4 The one clear exception was in relation to the question of willingness to accept any job to remain an organizational member. In this respect, the CECO manuals were the most 'highly committed' workforce, while the other three workforces exhibited 'low' levels of commitment. In considering this result in the context of our other findings, it appears that the question may have been interpreted differently by the manual and non-manual workforces in the four surveys, perhaps reflecting differing perceptions of their labour-market position. For example, findings from other questions in our survey suggest that the CECO manual workforce was more concerned about matters of job security than the other three workforces and had less knowledge of the current labour market for their skills. At the same time, it might be expected that their expectations as to autonomy and control over their work and career would be much lower than for the white-collar workforces, especially the technical employees at DECO and COCO. Accordingly, they might be expected to accept any job assignment

allocated to them by the employer, both because the alternative might be unemployment and because they would not perceive such an exercise of managerial prerogative as a threat to their careers. Conversely, the three non-manual workforces would not accept just any job the employer wished them to undertake since this might be perceived as undermining their career aspirations. Finding alternative employment in such circumstances would be seen as both desirable and viable. In short, we had strong doubts as to how far responses which declare a willingness to accept any kind of job to stay with the company could be interpreted unambiguously as indicative of high organizational commitment. Further statistical analysis again confirmed that we should drop this item in attempting to measure organizational commitment.

5 Guest and Dewe (1991: 78–9) also argue that it is a distinct outcome of organizational commitment and should not be confused with the process of being committed, as exhibited in attitudinal terms, by a desire to work hard for, or to maintain membership of, an organization. In other words, these factors should be seen as a consequence of a high level of identification with the organization. Our statistical analysis of the associations between the various commitment items confirms this view, and in our subsequent analysis we treated commitment to the organization's goals and values ('organizational identification') as separate from 'willingness to remain an organizational member'.

6

MANAGING CHANGE
WITHOUT UNIONS

This penultimate chapter extends our analysis of management style in non-union settings through an exploration of how technical and related organizational change was managed in our survey and case-study enterprises. In particular, we are concerned with the extent to which managers are better able to implement significant technical and related organizational change in the absence of unions. On the one hand, for example, non-union settings appear to have an inherent advantage when it comes to change since management is 'free' from the 'monopoly effects' associated with trade union presence. On the other, the absence of beneficial 'collective voice' effects may have to be compensated for if employees are to be adequately informed and their support gained. HRM suggests one means by which this might be achieved. As Clark (1993: 4–5) notes, with the adoption of HRM, technical and organizational change are meant to be part of the 'normality' of organizational life with personnel and industrial relations issues becoming a central strategic and operational consideration.

We begin by examining the findings from our postal and follow-up interview surveys of high-technology establishments. The remainder of the chapter then explores the nature of technical and organizational change, and the manner in which personnel and industrial relations issues highlighted by change were managed in our three case-study enterprises.

Technical change in the high-technology establishments

In Chapter 1 we noted that non-union establishments are less likely to have engaged in advanced technical change than their unionized counterparts. One of the objectives of our postal survey was to establish whether this was also the case in the supposedly highly innovative setting of the high-technology sector. In our follow-up interview survey we were also concerned with the implications of management style, particularly those of an HRM type, for the way personnel and industrial relations issues were considered when technical and organizational change took place.

Our postal survey findings, when compared to those of more general surveys (see, for example, Daniel, 1987; Northcott with Walling, 1988), revealed an above average level of innovation (see Table 6.1). However, on the key question of the effect of the presence or absence of recognized unions, our findings still reflected the more general picture painted by previous research. Thus, the establishments in the postal survey which recognized trade unions were more likely to have adopted microelectronics than the non-union establishments. Differences in establishment size and ownership did not effect this relationship, although smaller establishments (under 200 employees), whether unionized or not, were less likely to be users of new technologies than larger ones. When it came to the proportion of employees at the establishment working with new technology, there were no major differences between unionized and non-union establishments. However, plans to introduce new technology were more likely to exist in the non-union cases.

A more complex picture of the implications of the presence/absence of recognized unions emerged when related organizational change was taken into account (see Table 6.2). Overall, 40 per cent of the establishments that had introduced microelectronics had also made changes in working practices, supervisory

Table 6.1 Introduction of advanced technical change in the postal survey establishments (percentage of establishments)

	Union recognition		
	Union recognized	Non-union	All
Using advanced technology	96	81	84
Employees			
90–199	89	74	77
200+	100	93	96
Ownership			
British	92	85	87
Foreign	100	74	80
Proportion of workforce using advanced technology			
0–25%	35	37	36
26–49%	10	11	11
50–100%	50	48	49
Plan to use advanced technology	30	47	43

functions or management structures as a result. However, in general, this related organizational change appeared to have taken place slightly less often in unionized establishments, perhaps suggesting 'barriers' consequent on a 'monopoly effect'. When size of establishment was considered, it was evident that smaller non-union establishments (under 200 employees) were more likely to have implemented related organizational change than their similarly-sized unionized counterparts. However, in the case of larger establishments with 200 or more employees, it was those which recognized unions which were more likely to have made related organizational changes.

Our follow-up interview survey enabled us to take the analysis of change a step further by allowing a consideration of the question of management style. Two propositions suggested

Table 6.2 Introduction of technology-related organizational change in the postal survey establishments (percentage of establishments)

| | Union recognition | | |
	Union recognized	Non-union	All
Technology-related organizational change implemented	36	40	40
Employees			
90–199	12	40	37
200+	50	43	19
Ownership			
British	36	37	38
Foreign	36	44	42

themselves in this respect. First, the establishments we found with an HRM-type approach might be expected to be more likely to have undertaken technical change and to be using it more effectively through making technology-related changes in organization. One reason for this is that these establishments would be more likely to have the strategic involvement of specialist personnel managers, acting as either interventionary 'change-makers' or non-interventionary 'advisers' at an early stage in the change process (Storey, 1992: 168–9).

Second, those with non-HRM approaches would be less likely to have undertaken technical change and, if adopting, more likely to be using new technology at sub-optimum levels because they had not introduced technology-related organizational change. This, it could be suggested, would be because the lack of early specialist personnel involvement in change would mean the predominance of technical issues in the management of change which would be exclusively in the hands of line managers. How far did our findings confirm these propositions?

In fact, in terms of whether advanced technical change had occurred, there were no discernible differences between those establishments adopting an HRM-type approach and those adopting a different approach to the management of employee relations. Overall, 27 out of the 30 establishments in the follow-up survey had introduced advanced technology since 1980. Of the establishments not to do so, all had plans to introduce advanced technology over the next three years. Differences were more apparent, however, in respect of technology-related organizational change. Overall, 17 of the 27 establishments that had adopted advanced technology had also introduced related organizational change in at least one of our specified areas (job content, work organization and supervision). Establishments where an HRM approach was in evidence were slightly more likely (64 per cent against 52 per cent) to have introduced related organizational change in this way.

All but four of the follow-up survey establishments had personnel specialists on-site. However, in those with an HRM-type approach, specialist personnel involvement in change was more likely to be the norm, usually at an early stage, although this was more often as a provider of advice to line management rather than as a full-blown 'change-maker'. It is also worth noting that where personnel had not been involved at early stages in the past, there were in some cases plans to change this in the future.

In the case of the establishments with a non-HRM approach, there were also what appeared to be genuine examples of early and full personnel involvement, although again in the 'adviser' rather than 'change-maker' capacity. However, examples of more marginal involvement, and in some cases no involvement at all, were more evident. For example, in one establishment the personnel manager had not been involved in technical change even, it was claimed, when it concerned the computerization of the personnel department! In the main, therefore, change in these establishments appeared to be more exclusively in the hands of line management, with much less likelihood of significant personnel involvement. Moreover, the line-management role in these cases, at least as far as could be gleaned from the testimony of the personnel specialists who constituted our interviewees, was mainly technical.

In sum, the findings of our postal survey were consistent with earlier more broadly-based survey research which has suggested that unionized establishments are more likely to have undertaken advanced technical change than non-union establishments. Our follow-up interview survey suggested that the presence of HRM-type approaches was associated with technical change being accompanied by related organizational change. Moreover, it also appeared to be linked to a greater involvement of personnel specialists, if not as 'change-makers' then as 'advisors' to line management. Conversely, although there were exceptions, the absence of an HRM-type approach usually meant less personnel involvement in that the personnel specialism was either largely marginal or totally excluded from the change process. In these cases, line managers did not appear to be giving significant new attention to personnel and industrial relations issues.

Managing change at DECO, CECO and COCO

Our three case studies provide us with examples of technical and organizational change which, our survey findings would suggest, might be expected to have thrown up particular problems with regard to personnel and industrial relations matters. As we have seen, in none of the three enterprises was a full-blown HRM approach in evidence. It might be expected, therefore, that personnel and industrial relations issues were not likely to have been given particular prominence, and that line management would have played the dominant role in any technical and organizational change in the three enterprises. Moreover, their treatment of change as primarily a 'technical' issue might well have meant a neglect of key issues of this type such as communicating and consulting with employees or giving insufficient attention to technology-related organizational change.

We should note that our perspective on change in the case-study enterprises was somewhat broader than in our surveys. We were interested not only in technical change as exemplified by new technology and any related organizational change, but also in technology-driven changes in production methods and techniques, and major organizational changes which, at least in part, could be related to technical factors such as new product innovations. Our three case-study enterprises present different examples of technical and organizational change more broadly defined. In the case of DECO, the principal change involved the introduction of new technology in the form of an advanced CAD system. At CECO the main changes were constituted by a number of incremental innovations in production methods and quality-control techniques in the assembly of loudspeakers. In the case of COCO, major organizational changes were being driven by incremental innovations in its existing computer products and the introduction of new 'entry-level' machines.

In the case of DECO, training emerged as a major issue when the new technology was being implemented. Once fully operational, work organization and pay issues also came to the fore. At CECO, changes in the way loudspeakers were produced raised issues of pay and broad questions about changing the company culture to increase employee involvement and responsibility for quality. At the same time, discontent with the staff committee as a vehicle for communicating with employees and resolving grievances came to the fore. Finally, in the case of COCO, major changes in the way the business was organized highlighted the problem of lack of a coherent and formal personnel policy on matters such as pay determination and employee communications. Notably, in all three cases, line managers were the key 'change agents'. In the case of both DECO and CECO, personnel specialists were present but remained marginal. As we will see, in the case of COCO, the appointment of a personnel specialist was an integral but highly contested result of the changes taking place.

The introduction of CAD at DECO

One of the core features of DECO's business strategy was the aim to use CAD technology to secure competitive advantage. This had taken the form of a multi-million-pound investment in CAD which had begun at the end of 1981 when six terminals, linked to a mainframe computer, had been installed. By the end of the 1980s there were over 200 terminals in operation, linked to a far more powerful cluster of six mainframe computers. Moreover, even at the time of our study, some eight or nine years after the initial investment, new spending on CAD was still running at over £1 million a year.

Initially, the system had a mainly 2D capability. That is, CAD was used essentially as an electronic drawing-board to replace manual drawing using conventional pencils and T-squares. From 1986 far more sophisticated 3D modelling applications were developed. This involved 'test-building' an electronic model of the platform within the system, thus allowing any 'clashes' between components to be identified before fabrication (construction) began. The ability to produce a virtually 'clash-free' design was seen as the principal benefit of using CAD. This resulted in savings on rebuild costs incurred in the fabrication of the platform. By the end of the 1980s DECO had achieved net savings on overall project costs of up to 15 per cent which gave it a significant advantage over competitors when bidding for new projects. The company now claimed to be the world leader in the application of 3D CAD technology to offshore platform design.

However, despite the apparent success of this large investment and the lengthy period over which change had taken place, management, by its own admission, was only a short way up the 'learning curve' in respect of utilizing the system to its full potential. The reasons for this were partly technical in nature. However, a clear impression from our case study was that people issues had become increasingly prominent in DECO's attempt to adapt to the new technology. We can consider the way this had come about under the following headings: the approach taken to implementation; the implications of CAD for project management; and substantive issues of training, work organization and pay.

The approach to implementation was 'top-down' and backed by a high level of senior management commitment and support. The initial decision to adopt CAD had been made on the recommendation of a small group of senior engineering staff set up to conduct a feasibility study. A larger development team of 12 highly experienced engineers, seconded from each of the main discipline departments, was then created to install the chosen system. Subsequently this team provided the nucleus of a CAD Department which assumed responsibility for the development of the system and associated support services, including training. The head of the CAD Department emerged as the key change agent and promoter of CAD use in the company. The personnel specialism had no significant involvement in the initiation or implementation stages of change.

Little attempt was made by the development team to formally consult or inform employees. The main means of information disclosure was the somewhat informal device of training 12 'hand-picked' individuals and then dispatching them to their departments to 'sell CAD' by example. Given this, it is notable that in our employee survey, despite the vast majority being in favour of both technical and organizational change, exactly half of the DECO technicians said that management did not consult them 'very well' or 'at all well' about changes that directly concerned their job (see Table 6.3).

It was also the case that no questioning of management prerogative was tolerated. In fact, at the start of the implementation process there was a conscious decision to seek to minimize potential employee resistance by presenting CAD as a simple technical updating of equipment with no major implications for working or organization methods. However, subsequently CAD applications became more complex and changes in working methods and organizational arrangements more significant. At this point resistance from design engineers and middle managers to using CAD led the UK managing director to declare publicly: 'CAD is the future. CAD is the way we are going to do things. You can go out and tell anybody if they don't like it they can go.'

The principal personnel issue to be highlighted by the introduction of CAD was training. There was a shortage of trained staff within both the company and the industry as a whole. Moreover, there was also strong corporate pressure to show deliverable benefits from the investment. One tendency that existed in the selection of staff to be trained, therefore, was to choose the individuals 'most likely to be able to push the buttons'. Thus the immediate response was to concentrate on training younger and less experienced draughting technicians

Table 6.3 Employee attitudes to technical and organizational change (per cent)

	DECO	CECO		COCO
		Manual	Non-manual	
(a) Generally, how well do management consult you over changes that directly concern your job?				
Very well	5	6	14	6
Quite well	9	17	17	32
Just well enough	36	16	22	15
Not very well	34	36	42	34
Not at all well	16	25	6	12
(b) When new equipment is introduced are you:				
Strongly resistant to the idea of change	0	6	0	0
Slightly resistant to the idea of change	9	28	8	7
Slightly in favour of the idea of change	32	51	35	31
Strongly in favour of the idea of change	59	16	57	62
(c) When new organizational structures/working methods or ways of doing things are introduced, are you:				
Strongly resistant to the idea of change	0	7	0	0
Slightly resistant to the idea of change	11	30	8	31
Slightly in favour of the idea of change	41	46	41	39
Strongly in favour of the idea of change	48	16	51	30

who could quickly acquire sufficient competence as 'CAD operators' to undertake routine drawing and data-input tasks.

In the late 1980s the gradual extension of CAD to all major projects, together with the growth in more complex applications of the technology, served to highlight other significant areas of training need and pointed to weaknesses in the 'CAD operator' approach. For example, the limits of operator skills emerged as a constraint on the use of CAD where design experience was an important element of being able to use the technology effectively for more advanced 3D modelling of platform designs. As a result, training was extended 'upwards' to include higher-ranking design technicians. Similarly, it was also realized that a major error had been made in not providing professional engineers, project and discipline managers with sufficient technical appreciation of CAD to enable them to manage staff and projects effectively. Finally, the continued shortage of skilled labour meant that basic CAD training was also extended to sub-contract labour.[1] All this meant that, some eight years after initial adoption of CAD, training had grown into a substantial activity. The extent can be gauged by the fact that training courses lasted two weeks, with a further one-week top-up, and that up to 200 people undertook courses annually. Our employee survey confirmed that over 60 per cent of staff had received between two and five days' 'off-the-job' CAD training in the previous 12 months.

As already indicated, the introduction of CAD did not initially have a fundamental effect on working methods or organization. The main innovation had been that sketches and instructions for drawings had to be sent, in the manner of a typing-pool, to a centralized CAD centre for input by the CAD operators. In fact, this approach was modified very quickly since it acted to limit the use made of the system and exacerbated resistance to CAD among engineers and design technicians. Subsequently, CAD terminals were relocated to the offices in which the user projects were based. However, the introduction of more advanced CAD applications such as 3D modelling posed more fundamental questions, especially for the logic of the traditional division of labour between draughting and design technicians.

For example, in theory CAD freed *draughting* technicians from some routine and repetitive tasks which could be accomplished automatically and enabled them to engage in some elements of detail design. Three-dimensional modelling applications could also enable *design* technicians to develop detail designs directly on a terminal and thereby input their own information. This in turn could act to blur existing skill boundaries between engineering disciplines as both draughting and design technicians developed the 'composite skills' required to appreciate and interpret the consequences of their work for other disciplines. However, in practice, the extent to which new forms of work organization had emerged was patchy and tended to be project-specific.

The final personnel issue that arose concerned pay differentials between full-time and sub-contract staff. These were upset in two main ways. First, labour shortage meant sub-contract staff, who increasingly had CAD skills, could command a pay premium.[2] As a result, full-time, more highly-skilled designers found themselves supervising the work of lower-skilled sub-contractors operating the CAD system. Second, unlike under manual methods, it was no longer a straightforward task when, as one interviewee put it, 'the shit hit the fan' on a project, to increase output in order to meet a milestone. There was a limit on the amount of CAD hardware available, and justifying and acquiring additional workstations was not as easy as ordering a few extra drawing-boards from the stores. As a result, any 'peak working' on projects involved extending the working day (for example, through shift-working) so that additional workstation time could be created. Because this was difficult to anticipate in advance, such eventualities provided new opportunities for sub-contract staff to bargain a further pay premium through 'individual deals' with project managers.

In order to rectify this situation, just before our study began, full-time staff had been put on to six-monthly (as opposed to annual) pay reviews to allow catching-up. In addition, one effect of providing CAD training to full-time detail designers was to reduce the ability of sub-contract staff to claim a pay premium. That this was working to resolve any anomalies seemed to be corroborated by our employee survey of full-time design and draughting technicians. As noted in Chapter 5, this revealed a very high level of satisfaction with pay. It is also worth noting that almost all this group foresaw no difficulty in finding a job elsewhere if they decided to leave and said they would be prepared to quit if they became dissatisfied with their pay.

In sum, while in many ways the adoption of CAD at DECO was viewed as a success in technical and operational terms, it was clear that in personnel terms substantive issues such as training and pay had, to a significant extent, been reacted to after implementation once they had become 'problems', rather than anticipated and planned for in advance when the decision to adopt CAD was made and the system was being introduced. For example, seen through some managers' eyes, the diffusion of training to more and more constituents had been the result of trial and error and a response to crises on particular projects. On these occasions, 'man-hours' had to be thrown at projects to meet milestones which were in danger of being missed due to CAD-related problems. As extensive and expensive an investment as training had been, it was clear that, in many ways, lack of appropriate skills at detail-designer to middle-management level was still an important constraint on the effective use of the system. As one discipline manager summarized the current situation: 'we certainly are still not near the top of the learning curve in terms of managing the tool [CAD] from the point of view of getting the best out of it'.

Changes in production techniques at CECO

Despite the management buyout, the move to a new factory building, and major expansion in employment, no major investment in new production machinery had taken place at CECO. Indeed, most of the production equipment pre-dated the buyout in 1984. Technical change, as far as CECO was concerned, involved a series of incremental innovations in production methods and quality-control techniques which had, to date, occurred on a largely *ad hoc* basis. However, coupled to the move to the new factory, these added up to a substantial amount of change for the company. It is important to note that the key change agents were line management, in particular the manufacturing manager assisted by the production manager. The company quality manager was also important in attempting to move the company towards a 'Total Quality' approach. The personnel specialist, whose activity was largely administrative (see Chapter 4), had no role in the initiation or implementation of any of these changes, although she did become involved in supporting line management in resolving a number of issues concerning pay that arose as a result.

The overriding concern of the manufacturing and production managers in making changes to the production process was to increase throughput and productivity. It was also recognized that overhead and labour costs meant that more automation was needed on the shop-floor. However, knowledge of new production technology in the company was limited and investment funds were very tight. In addition, a previous experience of automation using 'pick and place' machines had not been successful, although a more recent investment of £20,000 in label-printing machines had proven more fruitful.

The first change in production methods had followed from the introduction of a new glue about six months before the start of our study. Despite the high technology involved in the design of loudspeakers, their production was relatively simple. As the manufacturing manager explained, speakers are 'just a metal cup, paper cone and a coil that moves, all held together by glue'. Previously, every speaker had to be assembled and set aside at each stage for the glue to dry. It therefore took three to four days to assemble a speaker. One disadvantage with this was that testing could only be done after a production run was complete. Thus, if a fault was identified the entire batch, sometimes of several thousand speakers, might have to be scrapped.

After some experiments with new 'fast curing' adhesives a suitable alternative was found that would allow 'straight-through manufacture'. This meant that gluing machines could be placed on the production lines and the layout of the shop-floor changed. Previously each line had been broken down into six segments spread around the factory. Now each line could run as a continuous sequence of tasks. This also allowed the testing of speakers during the production run. As a result, it now took 15 minutes to assemble a speaker and scrap rates had been reduced from around 8 per cent to 1.5 per cent.

In personnel terms, the immediate implication of this change was in relation to the bonus system which formed one element of shop-floor pay. Longer-term considerations concerning the need for a greater stress on output quality were also beginning to emerge. This challenged the prevailing production philosophy which required a detailed division of labour and tight monitoring and supervision of production work. Finally, these changes aggravated existing discontent among the manual work-force.

Before the change in production methods, an output-related bonus scheme had operated whereby individuals received a pay bonus linked to the number of speakers produced above a standard output rate. Although difficult for managers and employees alike to understand, the scheme had operated reasonably well with operators working in small groups on one of the six segments of the production lines. This had allowed the output from each segment to be more or less directly related to individual effort. The introduction of 'straight-through manufacture' meant that output could only be measured at the end of each production line and it was far more difficult for employees to predict their earnings for a given level of effort. As a result, they experienced large week-to-week fluctuations in take-home pay. This contributed to rising labour turnover and was a source of employee grievance; as part of an overall review of pay policy, the bonus scheme was eventually scrapped and replaced by a time-based payment system.

Alongside the move to 'straight-through manufacture' was an attempt to place greater emphasis on the quality of output. To this end, responsibility for quality during assembly had been passed from an inspection department under a quality manager to the manufacturing department. The quality manager was now encouraging manufacturing management to attempt to find ways of involving employees in monitoring the quality of their own output. A variety of quality-control techniques, including statistical process control, were in fact in use. For example, each loudspeaker was tested on the line by 'testers' (who were enclosed in a 'telephone booth' type workstation) during the production run. The results were displayed on a master board each hour, indicating where any problems were and how many rejects there had been. The objective was to reduce the figures for the next hour. If a defective speaker was found the previous hour's production was taken away for further inspection by the quality manager's staff. A daily assessment of the quality of the output of each line was also made and the results of this again displayed on the master board. Senior managers also met on a weekly basis to discuss output quality and the reasons for rejects.

Operators were also sometimes called in to discuss specific problems.

However, it was recognized that much of this activity, although primarily the responsibility of the manufacturing department, was still an 'after the event' exercise aimed at identifying problems before they left the factory. Other strategies for improving quality, sometimes ideas 'picked up' from other firms, had been tried with the intention of increasing employee responsibility for quality to prevent problems arising in the first place. Some visible evidence of this was provided by 'quality slogans' displayed on and around the shop floor. However, according to the production manager, attempts to involve employees tended to depend on the 'flavour of the month' in the sense of what was deemed appropriate given the climate of industrial relations at a particular time. For example, the current technique was 'walking the line' and asking operators about problems as part of a deliberate attempt to create a more 'open' management style. In the past, a form of 'quality circle' had been tried, known as the 'A-team'. This consisted of volunteers from each line who met under a team leader to try and find solutions to problems. The team operated for about a year and a half but collapsed because of labour turnover and criticisms from other line workers who identified the team members with the management. This kind of approach was not seen as appropriate at present and was being 'kept for another time'. A more modest idea currently being considered was a form asking operators 'What is there from stopping you doing your job better?'

According to the quality manager, the long-term aim was to move to a 'right first time' philosophy. However, in the context of an existing manufacturing philosophy which was output-orientated, there was a significant 'cultural problem' in requiring shop-floor staff to accept responsibility for quality, since this would result in a drop in production. Thus, in order to convince manufacturing management of the benefits, it was necessary to show how lower output could be offset by savings on scrap rates and rework costs. 'Winning this battle' was difficult. In addition, it was felt that the skills base on the shop-floor was probably too low and, even with training, many employees would not be able to take responsibility for quality. There was also a problem at supervisory level (see Chapter 4), but tight labour-market conditions meant the company had little room for manœuvre. Given these constraints, the aim at present was to try and reduce the number of problems finding their way into manufacturing from suppliers or through bad product engineering, and, in response to customer pressure, to gain BS 5750 approval. As the quality manager admitted, his vision of a 'Total Quality' culture in the company was 'still some way off'.

Finally, the manual employees were discontented with a number of aspects of their work. In particular, they were critical of working conditions in the new factory and health and safety hazards associated with the use of the new 'fast-curing' glue. These concerns were exacerbated, as the results of our workforce surveys revealed, by negative views of the utility of the staff committee. Indeed, on at least one occasion, shop-floor employees had apparently taken matters into their own hands and staged a 'walkout' to protest in the factory car park at the inadequate response to complaints about working conditions. It was noticeable, in this context, that the introduction of the new pay system had been accompanied by a more positive attempt by the staff committee representatives to develop a collective response to management proposals.

This discontent was not lost on management. Indeed, one reason why the staff association representatives were able to develop a more collective stance was that management deliberately invited the committee to play a more consultative role than hitherto. On the other hand, events such as the car park 'walkouts' tended to be seen by management as the female workforce having a 'fun day' and almost something to be encouraged to allow employees to 'let off steam'. In the main, the discontent among the manual workers was attributed by management to the amount of change they had been subjected to, rather than any substantive grievances with the changes themselves or the way they were managed. We can note, however, that the CECO manual employees were the least likely of our four workforces to view changes in technology or working methods favourably although, to be fair, the proportion who reacted to change negatively was still only in a minority (see Table 6.3).

Product innovation and organizational change at COCO

In the latter part of the 1980s a new business strategy had been formulated by COCO's US parent with the aim of expanding the customer base. The major feature of the strategy was a range of new, lower-cost, 'entry-level' versions of the large computer product. The new products were not only less expensive but also smaller, easier to maintain and offered greater 'connectivity' with other vendors' systems. In tandem with this programme of product innovation, it was also decided to stimulate renewed growth in revenue by targeting new markets in the chemical, pharmaceutical and financial services sectors.

The new markets were far more competitive. According to the head of marketing, this meant the company had to go out and actively sell its computers for the first time. At the same time, customer support had also to be given far more prominence and could no longer be viewed as 'just a side-effect of having sold equipment'. The new business strategy, therefore, required a move from a functional to a market-orientated organization structure to perform the company 'sales cycle'.[3]

Before reorganization, COCO was organized into five departments: Sales (including the field sales force), Technical Support, Engineering, the Data Centre, Software Development and Finance and Administration (see Figure 6.1). The Technical Support Department was split into marketing and software support groups. The new organizational structure involved the creation of two new departments. One was the Marketing and Sales Support Department, responsible for developing new and existing accounts. Within this department were marketing and technical experts drawn from the old Technical Support Department to support the sales force, in particular in 'qualifying' customers. The other was the Customer Service Department, created by combining the old Engineering Department with the remainder of the software experts from the Technical Support Department.[4]

Large COCO machines were normally sold with on-site hardware and software support, a typical installation having two technical specialists full-time at the customer location. The new

136

(a) Functional structure

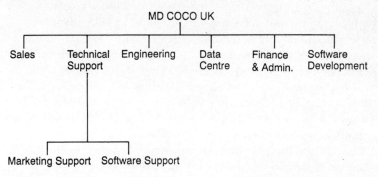

(b) Market-orientated structure

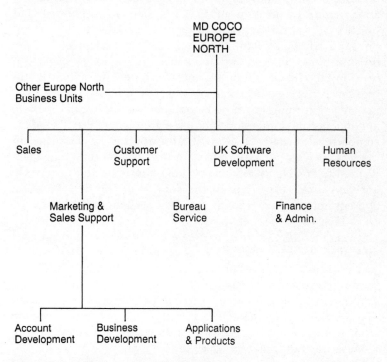

Figure 6.1 The shift from a functional to a market-orientated organization structure at COCO

Customer Service Department was intended to improve post-sales service by providing 'one-stop' maintenance (combining both hardware and software support) and to take advantage of the greater reliability of the new products. Increasingly maintenance tasks required composite software and hardware skills to diagnose problems and the equipment itself was capable of self-diagnosis. It was envisaged that this would enable reductions in the headcount of on-site staff, while the anticipated growth in the installed base of entry-level machines would allow a gradual move to cheaper off-site maintenance.

In implementing the new organization structure in the UK, a number of personnel and industrial relations issues were highlighted, not least the absence of a personnel specialism itself. One important consequence of these changes, therefore, was to bring home to senior management the lack of coherence, standardization and formalization in COCO's personnel policies and practice across different departments (see Chapter 4). Thus, during a strategic planning exercise which had preceded the organizational changes outlined above, the senior management team in the UK identified the need for a new 'people focus' in the company. In particular, it was felt that too much line-management time was now being spent on personnel matters and that, as the number of employees grew, there was a need for standardization and consistency in the application of policies on matters such as pay determination. In addition, line managers wanted to be able to 'ask complicated questions and get simple answers back', especially in the context of the new business strategy and products and the consequent changes to the way the workforce was to be organized.

It was therefore decided to create a new post for a personnel specialist. As an initial move towards improving the 'people focus' an external consultant was also commissioned to conduct a training-needs survey, the result of which was the introduction of a 'personal development' programme for senior and middle management. This included a variety of short courses ranging from 'team-building' to 'outward-bound' exercises (referred to by some as the 'nuts and berries' course!).

The new managing director, appointed after this exercise had been conducted, endorsed these developments wholeheartedly.

He commented to us that he was surprised to find no personnel specialism and the lack of basic personnel policies when he had arrived. Similarly, the new personnel manager, once appointed, was also surprised at the extent of neglect of personnel policy and that in some instances statutory requirements were not being observed. In her assessment there was a need to develop policies and improve practices in a number of areas, many of which had been highlighted as causes of staff discontent. For example, pay policy and employee communications had been singled out for immediate attention, especially in the light of the employee retention problems noted in Chapter 4.

One immediate change was a ruling by the new managing director that all salary increases had to be checked with the personnel manager. Another development was a number of additional initiatives to improve employee communications in the context of the changes that were taking place. According to the new managing director, there were a considerable number of management meetings but 'the thing that was clearly missing was anybody telling employees what was going on'. He therefore initiated two changes to produce what he described as an 'integrated system of communication'. First, managing director luncheons were held every four to six weeks for a dozen employees selected at random from all departments and also attended by the new personnel manager. These had an open agenda: the managing director briefed staff on any 'hot issues' and also invited matters of concern to staff or their colleagues to be raised. Second, team-briefing groups, intended as a forum for employees to express their views, were set up. However, there appeared to be some line-management resistance to this idea. After one round of briefings the process had been delayed until 'more support' could be given to line managers in conducting briefings. According to the personnel manager, 'it took some effort to even get them to happen. It's different to what some managers are used to in this company.'

Thus, by the time our study was completed at COCO in late 1990, the company had embarked upon a period of considerable change. At the same time, a new emphasis was being given to personnel matters, under the guidance of the new managing director and newly appointed personnel manager. Over the next

12 months it was planned to introduce a new appraisal scheme, conduct much more comprehensive work on comparative salary surveys in order to build up a database and, 'ideally', improve the computerization of personnel administration (despite the company's products the existing system was described as 'pretty abysmal'!). Another initiative current by the end of our study was the 'COCO Values Project Task Force', which had been set up in the UK to reassess the COCO 'style' statement in the light of the new business organization.

However, while there seemed to be broad agreement that the latest phase in the development of the company required a more effective administration of personnel matters, there was considerable concern among some senior line managers about how the new personnel activity was developing. In particular, there was a view that it had started to assume a policy-making role and, worst of all, was already expanding (a second specialist having been appointed to assist the personnel manager). Fears on this score had been heightened by a change in the reporting arrangements for the personnel function now named 'human resources', which was now the direct responsibility of the managing director.

One view was that this was a pragmatic solution to a short-term problem, following the departure of the director of finance and administration who had been the previous reporting point. However, at the same time, the personnel manager started to attend the weekly senior management group meetings. According to the personnel manager, the change occurred because it was thought that it would be easier to 'action policy' if she reported directly to the managing director and that, in any case, she had not been appointed as an administrator. In addition, direct reporting increased personnel awareness of business issues, 'allowing policies to be related more directly to the needs of the business and obviously the staff'.

Other members of the senior management team viewed the issue differently. One said that he and some of his colleagues had strong objections to the personnel manager 'being at their level' and 'sitting in on meetings' and suggested that this, on top of all of the other organizational changes, was having an adverse effect on morale among the senior managers. He claimed this was now very low: 'last Monday things were so fucking bad at least three

140

went down the pub and got completely smashed . . . people are pissed off'. In his view a personnel 'service' not 'direction' was needed.

Other members of the senior management team saw the issue more soberly. According to one, the senior management team supported the previous managing director's initiative in setting up a personnel function, but there was 'quite a lot of discussion about where that person should sit and whether she would be dictating personal policies or just helping the managers'. When we asked about this issue the managing director made it clear that he did not perceive the immediate task as being one of developing personnel strategies to cope with future developments in the company. However, it was recognized that the current changes in the business would highlight long-term issues which would eventually need to be addressed at this level. The task for now was to get 'all the basics right, and we're far from that'.

He also took the view that senior and many lower-level line managers were poor 'people managers' and that this was reflected in employees' perceptions. At the same time, the past experience of these managers was that they had managed their people well, a view endorsed perhaps by the previous managing director who was said to be 'strong on control but weak on organization'. The new managing director wanted a more 'open style' of management founded on a stronger organizational base. The personnel role was implicit in this, but some managers were finding it hard to adapt to the more open approach because of an 'in-built fear' of mistakes being identified. It is notable that the junior line managers we interviewed generally agreed with the new managing director's views on the need for a more professional approach to personnel matters, not least among middle and senior line managers.

Unlike our other two case studies, therefore, the personnel specialism at COCO was in fact central to much of the change that was taking place in the organization. Indeed, it had been brought into existence precisely because of issues highlighted by major organizational changes triggered by the new business strategy and product innovations. What is interesting here is the degree of conflict over not only who should have primary responsibility for personnel matters, but also what kind of personnel support was required. On the one hand, there were those among both middle and senior line management who insisted that, if required at all, the personnel specialism should merely play a non-interventionary role offering tactical advice to line managers. On the other, there was the view of the managing director that the role should, eventually at least, be both more interventionary and, if not strategic, at least advisory in orientation. Finally, the personnel specialist did not see her role as that of a 'handmaiden' (see Storey, 1992) servicing line management. Managing this set of diverse expectations was proving to be a major challenge for the individual concerned.

Finally, as in the previous cases, we should note the views from our employee survey on the issues of technical and organiz-ational change (see Table 6.3). On the question of technical change, as one might expect for a group of employees whose jobs were so directly related to bringing about such change in other organizations, the COCO computer staff were highly supportive. However, it is interesting to note that, on the specific matter of organizational change, nearly a third were prepared to say they were at least 'slightly resistant' to the idea of change. Finally, the new managing director's concerns regarding employee com-munications are borne out to the extent that just under half said that management did not consult them 'very well' or 'at all well', over changes which directly concerned their work. It should also be noted, however, that our survey also took place before most of the new employee communications initiatives had begun to be implemented in full.

Conclusion

This chapter has been concerned with the question of technical and related organizational change in non-union settings. The findings from the postal survey suggested that unionized estab-lishments were more likely to adopt advanced technology than non-union establishments, although this pattern was not so clear when it came to related organizational change. The follow-up interview survey also indicated that technical change was more likely to be accompanied by related organizational changes where HRM-type approaches were evident. In these cases personnel specialists appeared to have a greater involvement, albeit usually as an 'adviser' rather than 'change-maker'.

In each of our case-study establishments line managers were the main promoters of change, and personnel specialists played a marginal role. However, this occurred in the absence of a fully-fledged HRM approach, and the preoccupations of line management were predominantly technical. This resulted in 'people problems' of varying degrees of magnitude in each case. In only one case, that of COCO, could change and the people issues it highlighted be said to have acted as a catalyst for a broad review of how the firm approached managing its employees. In short, managing change without unions was, in personnel and industrial relations terms, far from problem-free in our three case-study enterprises.

Notes

1 This was part of an industry-wide initiative in conjunction with a local college and supported by funds from the Engineering Industry Training Board and Manpower Services Commission.

2 It should be noted that the acquisition of CAD skills by sub-contract staff not only came about by the extension of training to cover them. It was also a function of the standard practice of full-time staff electing to switch to sub-contract status at certain points in their career. In theory, therefore, a technician on a full-time contract could be trained by DECO to use CAD, and then go on to sub-contract terms and offer their services back to the company at a premium. In recognition of the growth of this practice the company introduced a ruling that former full-time employees could not be re-employed by the company on a sub-contract basis until a period of six months had elapsed.

3 The COCO sales cycle began with 'lead' activities designed to identify potential customers and stimulate interest in and awareness of the company's products. Once identified, the next step was to 'qualify' customers by establishing their business needs and financial capabilities. Subsequent pre-sales stages involved more detailed technical proposals, 'closing the deal' and the signing of contracts. Once shipped and installed, post-sales activities involved growing the business by providing technical support and helping customers identify new business needs. The minimum period for the sales cycle

was about six months and the maximum five years. The average cycle lasted two to three years. One recent sale was the result of ten years of contact with a firm!

4 With the creation of these new departments, the Data Centre was renamed the Bureau Service, with the emphasis placed on the selling of computer time on a more commercial basis to both potential and existing customers.

7

CONCLUSION: TOWARDS A NON-UNION SYSTEM?

This book has been concerned with the hitherto largely neglected topic of non-unionism and the non-union firm. In Chapters 1 and 2 we set out to place our research in the context of the decline of trade union organization, the debate over management style, and the emergence of new HRM techniques as a potential non-union alternative to managing industrial relations. The remaining chapters reported findings from our own study of the non-union phenomenon as it is manifested in the high-technology sector in the South East of England.

We were concerned in particular with three main issues: the nature of management style; the attitudes of non-union employees; and the management of change, especially technical and related organizational change. We begin this concluding chapter by summarizing our findings under these three headings. We then broaden our discussion to address some of their implications in the context of contemporary trends in 'union-free' industrial relations in Britain. Finally, we consider three scenarios for the future development of non-union industrial relations.

Management style in the non-union firm

How do non-union firms manage their industrial relations and to what extent are new HRM techniques prevalent? Our choice of the high-technology sector as the focus for our study was largely guided by this question since many commentators have associated it with a predominantly non-union approach and seen it as being populated by many of the leading exponents of HRM.

In Chapter 2, HRM was defined in conceptual terms as a management style which could be contrasted with traditional personnel management practice. Following Guest (1987) and Storey (1992), HRM was characterized as a combination of interdependent personnel policies which were closely linked to overall business strategy and line-management practice and which were designed to secure employee commitment, high performance, flexibility and innovation. Two variants of HRM were identified: 'soft' versions, which stressed the *human* aspect of managing human resources, the focus being on developing competent and committed employees; and 'hard' versions, where the focus was on optimizing the utilization of human *resources* in a dispassionate and formally rational manner.

It was also suggested that to the extent that HRM is based on unitary values, it may well be inconsistent with trade unions and collective bargaining. However, the extent to which this was so depended upon the particular variant of HRM being discussed. 'Soft' variants, or 'traditional HRM', were, for example, likely to view investment in human resources as leading to a reduction in demands for trade union services on the part of employees. 'Hard' variants, or 'strategic HRM', would be more open to evaluating the relevance of trade unions and collective bargaining in the context of finding the most appropriate competitive strategy in given product- and labour-market conditions.

To aid the subsequent discussion of our empirical findings we suggested that management style in non-union settings could be conceptualized in terms of two analytically distinct dimensions: first, the degree of 'strategic integration' between individual personnel policies and between these and overall business strategy; second, the balance between individual and collective methods of regulation in relation to particular substantive and procedural aspects of the employment relationship.

The resulting schema suggested four broad approaches. First, those which combined high levels of strategic integration with a pronounced preference for individualistic approaches to managing the employment relationship ('traditional HRM'). Second, those which combined high levels of strategic integration with a contingent mix of collective and individual regulation ('strategic HRM'). Third, those where policies and practices were more reactive and pragmatic and were combined with a preference for individualized employment relationships in the context of a degree of employer dependence on the skills of the employee ('benevolent autocracy'). Fourth, those where a pragmatic and reactive approach was combined with an opportunistic mix of individual and collective regulation ('opportunists').

Finally, we also noted the importance of contingent factors, in particular product-market pressures, in shaping management style. It was suggested, following Marchington and Parker (1990), that the power of the product market to influence the way labour is managed is largely shaped by two factors: the degree of competitive pressure and the degree of customer pressure. The greater the product-market pressure the less room for manœuvre managers will perceive themselves as having in the way they manage employees, and the more likely it is that their approach will stress the managerial prerogative. Conversely, the weaker such pressures, the more management can exercise discretion and choice regarding such matters, and the more able they may be to develop an HRM-type approach.

In Chapter 3 the findings from our postal and follow-up interview surveys suggested the following. First, although we found a relatively high level of non-unionism in the high-technology sector in South East England, the influence of HRM-type approaches was relatively limited. However, notable examples of 'traditional HRM' were identified in some non-union settings. In the main, there was considerably more variation in how management chose to manage employees without unions, with examples of 'benevolent autocracy' particularly prevalent but also more opportunistic and pragmatic attempts at 'union avoidance'. Notably, the few instances where unions had been derecognized appeared to be characterized by the latter approach.

The type of management style did not appear to be strongly determined by the nature of product-market pressures. In most cases these were sufficiently weak to allow management a reasonable amount of latitude. Having said this, it was clear that changes in the product market had, in some cases, acted as an external impetus to review personnel and industrial relations practices. Finally, equally important in this respect was the nature of the labour market. Shortage of suitably qualified employees and the devising of effective means to recruit, reward and retain them, were often far more of a problem than a surfeit of competitors or a shortage of customers. Indeed, many managements appeared to perceive labour-market shortages as the strongest constraint and the factor most likely to influence attempts to change the way employees were managed.

The absence of a fully-fledged HRM-type approach was also a feature of our findings in the three case studies presented in Chapter 4. As such, we suggested that these three enterprises provided what were perhaps more typical examples of non-unionism than those of the much vaunted HRM type. In none of them was there strong evidence of high levels of 'strategic integration'. In the case of DECO and CECO, personnel policies were relatively formalized but the personnel function had a purely administrative role. However, at COCO the situation was more complex. While the corporate policy statements of the US parent appeared to fit a 'traditional HRM' model, and despite elements of this approach being evident at COCO (UK) in the 'COCO Style Statement', this did not appear to have a defining influence on actual managerial behaviour. The espoused style statement acted at best as a 'background' influence, and in reality only a basic formalization of personnel policies was evident, with little integration between specific policies or with overall business policy. In this context, UK line managers were relatively free to formulate their own idiosyncratic approaches to managing industrial relations and related personnel matters.

In the absence of unions, the management styles of both COCO and DECO placed a great stress on the individual nature of the employment relationship, particularly in relation to pay determination, but also in communications with employees and grievance handling. CECO was rather different in so far as it had a previous history of union recognition. The decision to dere-cognize appeared to be an opportunistic one, consistent with a predominantly pragmatic approach to personnel and industrial relations matters, which left open the possibility of union recognition in the future. Management claimed derecognition had been a success and, as at COCO and DECO, the absence of unions was now viewed as a reflection of the fact that employees saw no need for them. Significantly, however, at CECO many of the trappings of a collective approach to managing the employ-ment relationship had been retained. This was most obviously so not only in institutional terms – for example the staff committee and other personnel policies – but also in the more subtle sense of the way managers perceived the employment relationship, defined its attendant 'problems', and prescribed what they felt were appropriate 'solutions'.

As in our survey, we also tried to relate the way in which employees were managed in the three case-study enterprises to the particular product-market conditions they faced. The greatest constraint on freedom to act was perceived by DECO manage-ment. They saw a highly individualized and union-free approach to managing their workforce as the only way to achieve business objectives in a competitive product market. Demand was highly cyclical and the contract-based nature of the work undertaken brought with it high levels of customer pressure. Conversely, the high market share and strong growth enjoyed by COCO ap-peared to support a greater degree of freedom for its UK managers in choosing how they managed their employees. In addition, as we noted in Chapter 6, in responding to increased product-market pressure, COCO management was able to move to address deficiencies in the way personnel matters were dealt with in a manner which suggested an, albeit limited, move in the direction of HRM.

In the case of CECO, rather acute product-market pressures had surrounded the management buyout and these were clearly seen to leave management with little choice in derecognizing the unions. However, subsequent business success meant that these pressures had, in relative terms, relaxed. As a result management was beginning to think more pragmatically about the possible future trade union organization of the workforce. Unlike their counterparts at DECO and COCO, managers at CECO did not have a long history of viewing trade unions as fundamentally inconsistent with the kind of business strategy that was required to succeed in their product market.

Employees in the non-union firm

Obviously, a reliance on managerial perceptions of the nature and conduct of industrial relations in non-union settings runs the strong risk of giving a one-sided picture of reality. Our second main concern was therefore with employees' attitudes in non-union firms, and in particular the question of why they did not join unions. This turned out to be a particularly pertinent question in our three case-study enterprises since there were very few union members among the workforces that we surveyed.

We suggested three potential reasons why employees in non-union settings might not join unions. First, non-membership may be a function of a withdrawal of support for trade unions consequent of a decline in collective and a rise in individualistic attitudes among employees and in society at large. Second, the lack of an available union to join at a workplace might explain low levels of union membership among employees who are predisposed to join. Finally, management policies of an HRM type could be expected to result in a reduction in employee demands for union services due to their increased commitment to organizational goals and values. The evidence we presented suggested that the lack of union availability explained non-union membership in only one of our four surveyed workforces, the CECO manual workers. These employees exhibited a propensity to join which was frustrated by the lack of an available union to join. In this instance union presence may well have resulted in favourable employee attitudes being accompanied by union-joining behaviour. This conclusion was given considerable support by other evidence from the CECO case study, which pointed to an emergent collectivization among both employees and their staff committee representatives.

What was surprising about this finding was that these were not the views of a hitherto well-organized traditional manual workforce. Although derecognition had taken place at CECO, much of the old workforce had been made redundant. The workforce, which now exhibited a high propensity to unionize, had many of the characteristics of 'new workers' normally seen as resistant to unionization. For example, the majority of CECO manuals were young, had limited labour-market experience, had little previous experience of union membership, and the vast majority were women.

However, in the case of the non-manuals at CECO, the DECO technicians and the COCO computer staff, lack of an available union to join did not appear to explain non-membership. For most of these employees, and this was again supported by our other case-study evidence, union presence would apparently have largely made no difference. However, neither did their propensity to unionize appear to be an attitudinal outcome related to management styles which might have been expected to reduce demands for union services and engender high levels of organizational commitment. While these employees were, in the main, fairly satisfied with their jobs, had mainly positive views of non-union voice mechanisms provided by management, and were reasonably committed to the organization, our statistical analysis did not identify these factors as the key motivation for not joining a union.

Rather, propensity to join a union appeared to have more to do with instrumental and ideological beliefs about unions than with attitudinal outcomes that might be anticipated as the consequence of HRM-type approaches. Perhaps management did not necessarily need to set about reducing demands for union services among the DECO technicians, CECO non-manuals and COCO computer staff because these employees had little inclination towards making such demands in the first place.

The management of change in the non-union firm

Our final research issue concerned the management of technical and related organizational change in non-union settings. On the one hand, non-union settings appear to have an inherent advantage since they are 'free' from the 'monopoly effects' associated with trade union presence. On the other, the absence of beneficial 'collective voice' effects may have to be compensated for if employees are to be adequately informed and their support gained. HRM may be important in this respect since its adoption suggests that such change is part of the 'normality' of organizational life. Moreover, personnel *issues* become a central strategic and operational consideration, although it is a moot point whether personnel *specialists* themselves have a more central role.

The evidence from our surveys and case studies did not give strong support for the view that, in itself, being non-union confers an advantage when it comes to technical change. Our postal survey, consistent with broader-based evidence from other research, suggested that unionized establishments were more likely to adopt advanced technology than non-union establishments. On the question of the influence of HRM-type approaches, our findings did indicate that technical and related organizational changes were more likely in settings where this approach was evident. However, it was notable that this tended to mean personnel specialists had greater, rather than less, involvement, albeit usually as 'advisers' rather than 'change-makers'.

The three case studies provide examples of how the arguably more typical non-union enterprise manages technical and organizational change. In each case, line managers were the principal promoters of change, but in the main their preoccupations were predominantly technical. This resulted in problems of varying degrees of magnitude in each case. At DECO these were the result of a largely reactive approach to training and other personnel issues in the context of the introduction of new CAD technology. At CECO they reflected the limits imposed by a pragmatic and output-orientated production philosophy which did not actively engage employee support for change and was inconsistent with the first steps being taken towards a 'Total Quality' culture. Finally, at COCO they revolved around 'technology-led' line managers with a deep suspicion of personnel specialists and the difficulties this caused in getting them to accept that a personnel function had a legitimate role to play in an enterprise undergoing major product innovations and related organizational change.

Of course, none of this adds up to a conclusion that union presence is necessarily advantageous when it comes to introducing technical and organizational change. However, neither does it add substance to the view that union absence is an automatic advantage. Indeed, the approach to managing employees in our case-study enterprises, coupled with the evidence from our postal and interview surveys, strongly suggested that change of a broad variety of kinds without unions is far from 'problem-free' in personnel and industrial relations terms.

'Union-free' industrial relations: how typical is 'high tech'?

Our study has focused on the high-technology sector. This obviously raises the question of how far our findings are typical of the non-union sector as a whole. Certainly, the image of the high-technology sector as one where managing without unions is based on HRM, would suggest that it is unlikely to be typical of other sectors of the economy which have low levels of union organization.

The WIRS 1990 survey allows us to make a judgement here since it provides some important clues to the *general* characteristics of 'union-free' industrial relations at workplace level. Moreover, the authors of the survey imply that their findings would describe much of industrial relations in the private sector should, as some predict, trade union organization and collective bargaining become increasingly confined to the public sector and a small proportion of traditional manufacturing industry (Millward *et al.*, 1992; Millward, 1994).

According to the WIRS survey, the main characteristics of 'union-free' industrial relations are as follows. First, 'employee voice' in non-union settings is more circumscribed, irregular and informal than in the unionized sector. For example, much less information is provided to employees by management and there are fewer formal channels for information disclosure and

153

consultation. There are also fewer formal grievance and disciplinary procedures, and labour turnover is higher.

Second, in terms of pay the link between the market and individual performance is more directly drawn. Pay is more likely to be determined by the ability to pay, rather than by other social or comparability criteria, and to be related to individual performance. Pay differentials are wider and more employees are on 'low pay'. However, while pay is set unilaterally by management, a minority of non-union workplaces do consult employees or their representatives about pay increases.

Third, industrial relations have few of the trappings of industrial conflict and its management. There are virtually no strikes and absenteeism is no worse. Personnel specialists are less likely to be present and managers are more likely to perceive the industrial relations 'climate' in positive terms – although employee morale is more likely to be seen as an issue. Fourth, job security is significantly weaker, with the likelihood of compulsory redundancies being greater, the incidence of dismissals higher, and the use of non-standard employment contracts more widespread. Finally, the management prerogative is more marked. Managers feel less constrained in the way they organize work but the physical working environment is less well regulated, there being fewer health and safety representatives and more accidents and injuries.

Our findings from the high-technology sector do not provide such a 'bleak house' (Sisson, 1993: 207) picture of non-unionism. However, neither do they provide strong evidence of an 'alternative' model of non-unionism based around HRM. In fact, our results suggest that the reality of non-union industrial relations in the high-technology sector lies somewhere between these two extremes. For example, while employee voice was circumscribed in many settings and pay did tend to be determined by management unilaterally, we also found plenty of evidence of how individual employees in strong labour-market positions could exert a measure of control over their own circumstances. In particular, to the extent that management approach could be characterized as 'benevolent autocracy', there was a recognition of dependence upon employees with scarce labour-market skills which were essential to the business. In such instances, management style, whether it was 'looking after the wives' as at DECO, or 'laughter in the halls' and a 'small-firm' feel as at COCO, recognized the need to 'carry the support of employees' if business objectives were to be achieved. Even if the methods for achieving this were sometimes highly informal, if not rudimentary, they did not amount to the unhindered or unconstrained exercise of the managerial prerogative. In contrast, at CECO, the employment relationship was clearly seen by management and the workforce in adversarial terms, and this found collective expression through forms of industrial conflict more commonly associated with unionized settings.

Our findings would therefore lead us to suggest that, although hardly typical in all of the terms described by the WIRS survey, the forms of industrial relations we found in the high-technology sector are not so far removed as to make the sector a 'one-off' or 'atypical' case. Indeed, our overall conclusions are not too far removed from those reached by the authors of the WIRS survey themselves with regard to the non-union sector as a whole (Millward *et al.*, 1992: 365):

> All this suggests that employee relations in non-union, industrial and commercial workplaces had relatively few formal mechanisms through which employees could contribute to the operation of their workplace in a broader context than their specific job. Nor were they as likely to have opportunities to air grievances or to resolve problems in ways that were systematic and designed to ensure fairness of treatment. Broadly speaking, no alternative models of employee representation – let alone a single alternative model – had emerged as a substitute for trade union representation.

Implications for trade unions

From reading the list of characteristics of non-union workplaces identified by the WIRS 1990 survey, it might be concluded that unions would have considerable grounds for optimism in recruiting in non-union firms. Compared to their unionized counterparts, for example, employees are more likely to be subject to arbitrary managerial authority, have low pay, less job security and, apart perhaps from quitting, no means to air their grievances. Moreover, our findings suggest that HRM strategies are not typical in high-technology settings and that a strong 'union substitution' effect is not the main reason for the absence of unions. Suppose, then, trade unions were to renew their ambitions to expand the membership base into relatively weakly organized areas such as the high-technology sector. To what extent would this offer a potentially fruitful recruiting ground, or do our findings support the view that the sector is effectively a 'no-go' area for unions?

As far as employee attitudes are concerned, if the emerging collectivism among the CECO manual workforce is taken as indicative, then there may well be circumstances where employees judge that a union would provide them with a better chance of protecting and advancing their interests than is possible if they go it alone as individuals. However, employee attitudes of this type are unlikely to be typical of the high-technology sector as a whole. By virtue of their labour-market position and employer dependence on their skills, employees are not, as individuals, completely defenceless. Moreover, such employees may not see their employer as particularly 'bad', or have a view of trade unions, whether based on past membership experience or not, as relevant to them when it comes to determining their pay and conditions and protecting their jobs. Our workforce surveys at CECO (non-manuals), DECO and COCO indicated that employees could enjoy sufficient advantage from their employment, in terms of not only remuneration, but also the satisfaction that they gained from the content of their work, to make instrumental judgements that they 'did not need' a union appear genuine.

In circumstances such as these, if recruitment is to be successful, union membership will have to be 'sold' to potential members as something more than a collective defence against the actual experience of an unscrupulous employer, uncompetitive pay, poor working conditions or job loss. Rather the emphasis will have to be on the marketing of a wider range of services, such as financial and legal services, which offer 'insurance' to individual members, together with the adequate resourcing as well as the prioritization of such recruitment strategies (Mason and Bain, 1991; Bassett and Cave, 1993). The problem, as Kessler and

Bayliss (1992: 270) observe, is that 'British trade unions are not used to recruiting members by the same methods as the Automobile Association.'

Of course, gaining new members in the high-technology sector would only be the first step for trade unions. They would also eventually be faced with the task of winning recognition from employers. On the plus side, our evidence suggests that even in a sector such as high technology, non-union employers do not appear to have found universally applicable solutions to the problem of managing without unions. This does not mean that non-union employers are about to invite union recognition as a potential means of resolving their industrial relations difficulties. However, it does suggest that many of the situations in which employers seek to sustain or move to non-union status may hold some hope for unions. This is because employers may have sought to remain, or aim to become, 'free' of unions in an opportunistic and pragmatic manner, possibly with a false perception of what managing a workforce without unions might entail as the firm matures and the workforce expands. For such employers – and CECO could be regarded as indicative – managing without unions could conceivably turn out to be as troublesome as managing with them, if not more so.

On the other hand, in general the 'employer market' for union services has clearly become increasingly hostile (Willman *et al.*, 1993). Such reluctance to see the worth of trade union presence may be particularly entrenched among management in high-technology firms who would see any demand for union services by their employees as an indication of their own 'failure'. Thus, at best, unions might well find themselves restricted in many of these firms just to marketing individual membership services, which are not dependent upon employer recognition of the union, without any realistic prospect of such recognition ever being forthcoming.[1]

The findings of our employee surveys also point to an additional consideration for unions with ambitions to seek to expand their membership base into relatively unorganized areas. An approach advocated by the TUC has been to launch 'blanket' recruitment campaigns in geographically defined labour markets (TUC, 1988; 1989). We would venture to suggest that this runs the risk of being very 'hit and miss' unless the labour-market intelligence upon which it is based is highly detailed and specific. If not, a possibility is that relatively large amounts of resources, which might have been better utilized in a more focused campaign, could be committed to organize employees with a low propensity to unionize. For example, assuming our three case-study enterprises were located in a local labour market targeted for recruitment efforts, the manual employees at CECO might have been highly receptive to the message of such an initiative, while the non-manuals and the employees at DECO and COCO would, on the basis of our findings, largely have been hostile.

This suggestion can be put into the broader context provided by the British Social Attitudes Surveys conducted during the 1980s. In their review, Dibden and Millward (1991: 15–16) report that, while for a minority of non-union members some of the reasons given for non-membership suggest a potential for union recruitment, for most non-union members the question of why they were not in a union was 'simply not salient'. Of course, this begs the question of how unions are to identify non-union locations and workforces where employees do have a high propensity to unionize.

All of this points to the likely difficulties for trade unions in both identifying and attracting new members in circumstances where a higher priority and far more resources are likely to be required to sustain successful recruitment campaigns than in the past. If our four workforces are anything to go by, even given a potentially attractive and appropriately targeted package of membership services, unions will still need to research their membership 'markets' carefully in order to make sure that recruitment resources are not wasted on 'lost causes'.

Towards a non-union system?

This brings us, finally, to the point at which we began, the context for non-unionism and the non-union firm provided by contemporary trends in the British system of industrial relations. In Chapter 1 we outlined some of the key changes. We noted, for example, that legal changes have given employers much greater capacity to marginalize, or even choose to manage without, unions, while product-market and other environmental pressures which might trigger such a process have also increased. At the same time, much appeared to have changed in relation to union membership and density, union recognition, and the coverage and structure of collective bargaining, all of which pointed to a decline in the significance and influence of trade-union-based industrial relations. However, these changes were not explained by a wholesale rejection of trade unions and collective bargaining on the part of employers, managers and employees. The effect of the legal changes, for instance, was far from clear-cut and factors such as recession, plant closure and redundancy appeared to explain much of the decline observed. As such, the rise of non-unionism and the non-union firm was more a consequence than a cause of the decline of trade unions and collective bargaining.

What, then, are the likely future trends in the final years of the twentieth century? Will the British system undergo a 'transformation' of the type experienced in the USA? Will a coherent non-union alternative emerge to supplant trade unions and collective bargaining? Or will the basic institutional framework continue to survive in a much shrunken but otherwise relatively unscathed unionized sector? Indeed, given more favourable economic, political and legal support, might the trade unions, armed with new 'member-friendly' policies, be able to recruit sufficient new members to secure recognition in the growing unorganized sectors?

Needless to say, the answers to such questions can only be determined by events. Nevertheless, we can suggest three broad, not entirely mutually exclusive, scenarios within which the significance of the non-union phenomenon might be judged in the future. The first suggests that, despite some apparent appearances to the contrary, 'decollectivization' has already – albeit in an uneven and incremental fashion – 'transformed' the industrial relations system. On the one hand, while admittedly diminished in coverage and scope, unions and collective bargaining still have a significant presence and the institutions of joint regulation remain more or less intact. However, on the other, the actual attitudes and behaviour of the parties is such as to render

159

this institutional framework no more than an 'empty shell'. In reality, the frontier of control has shifted so far in management's direction that unions are now able to offer only token resistance as their members gradually drift away and union organization 'withers on the vine'. There has in essence been 'an end to institutional industrial relations' (Purcell, 1993), whereby 'the traditional, distinctive "system" of British industrial relations' is no longer characteristic of the economy as a whole (Millward *et al.*, 1992: 350).

Chief architect in this process is the Conservative government and its continuing reform of the legal framework within the context of a 'presumption of non-unionism' (Smith and Morton, 1994: 11). This has given employers an increasing capacity to decollectivize the employment relationship, and has severely undermined the capacity of trade unions to resist such that 'the new industrial relations is characterised by employer-regulated organisation-employment systems utilising cost minimisation strategies devoid of any systematic HRM content, with no or reduced union input' (Smith and Morton, 1994: 11). Within this scenario, without radical political and economic changes favourable to trade unions (which the return of a future Labour government is not seen as guaranteed to promote), non-unionism and the non-union firm are set to increase in importance as a key characteristic of future industrial relations in Britain.

A second scenario points to the 'stickiness' rather than the 'hollowness' of industrial relations institutions and the pattern of behaviour they support among the parties. In the early part of the 1980s this 'stickiness' was sufficient to support arguments of stability, continuity and little change, despite the assault from the environment (Batstone and Gourlay, 1986; Millward and Stevens, 1986; Batstone, 1988; MacInnes, 1988; Kessler and Bayliss, 1992). In this view a short, in historical terms at least, period of government by a party whose rhetoric was hostile to trade unions, is insufficient to undermine the embedded and encrusted attitudinal and behavioural patterns of management, unions and employees. Previous examples of supposedly transformational change could be pointed to – the 1971 Industrial Relations Act, for instance – which failed to have the intended effect on the British industrial relations system (Beaumont,

1990: 257). Indeed, the surprising thing about the period since 1979 is not that the system has been transformed, but rather that the change that has undoubtedly occurred has been far more limited than might have been expected in a period when management has been so much in the ascendancy (Kessler and Bayliss, 1992: 265).

In a more sophisticated version of this thesis, which avoids the accusation of a preoccupation with institutions rather than the reality of the actions of the parties, Dunn (1993) points to the rigidities in the way management frames and perceives its own responses and actions. He suggests that the post-Donovan formalization of collective bargaining institutions and the position of trade union representation within enterprises led to an 'incorporation' of management into thinking which suggested that trade unions and collective bargaining were a necessary part of any prescription to solve the problems that businesses faced. In the 1980s, notwithstanding some significant superstructural damage, the survival of the institutions of joint regulation owes much to these difficulties and the problems management has subsequently had in articulating and sustaining alternatives which do not involve trade unions and collective bargaining. The problem for management, as Dunn (1993: 179) puts it, has been to 'deincorporate' themselves and unload much of the institutional 'baggage' associated with the post-Donovan 'formalization' of collective industrial relations. This they have only managed to do in a 'creeping' fashion. Indeed, the case of CECO would seem to provide a particular manifestation of this phenomenon. In this scenario, therefore, the long-term significance of non-unionism and the non-union firm is less obvious. Indeed, in the end, for the cautious 'post-Donovan' manager, HRM and non-unionism may present too radical, risky and, above all, costly an alternative.

The final scenario presents the most positive prognosis for non-unionism and the non-union firm. This suggests that a return to the free-market principles of previous epochs, albeit in a guise appropriately updated for modern conditions, represents the inevitable way forward for industrial relations. This 'back to basics' view points to the liberation of employers and employees from the tyranny of constraint imposed by trade unions and the supportive legal and public policy framework erected, in particular, in the 1970s. The latter view has, of course, been expressed in the rhetoric of the Conservative government which is prone to equate the growth of non-unionism and the decline of collective bargaining with a more educated workforce and the 'modernization' of the economy (see, for example, Department of Trade and Industry, 1990). The notion of new benign and enlightened HRM techniques fits neatly into this line of reasoning.

In this scenario, apart from the increasingly anachronistic remnants of the public sector and a few pockets of 'rustbelt' industry in the private sector, non-unionism and the non-union firm represent a future of employment growth in the context of labour-market flexibility. Proponents argue that there *have* been fundamental and deep-seated changes in attitudes and that 'fewer employees – and employers – feel the need of union mediation in their dealings'. Hence, the presumption of the past that trade union organization and collective bargaining should be extended to new and expanding parts of the economy is no longer justified. In short, 'collective bargaining no longer presents itself as the only or even the most obvious method of handling relations at work' (Gilbert, 1993: 252).

Implicit in all of these views is some sense of significant change in industrial relations. The real question now is not whether change has occurred, but rather to what extent and in what directions it will develop. It is not inevitable that we have to 'go back' to get to 'the future'. One mould, to coin a phrase, may have been broken, but a new one has yet to be set. It remains to be seen whether a coherent non-union alternative will emerge in Britain, especially now that the non-union sector is more prominent and its organization by trade unions apparently more problematic.

Concluding comment

At the beginning of this book we noted one commentator's observation that there remains a very full agenda awaiting industrial relations researchers with regard to non-unionism and the non-union enterprise. We cannot claim to have exhausted this agenda in our exploratory forays into the non-union firm and the attitudes and behaviour of managers and employees therein. Indeed, in the final part of this chapter we have sought to stimulate debate rather than provide definitive answers. However, we do hope that our findings and the questions we have posed will encourage others to join in the investigation of this hitherto neglected but increasingly significant area of industrial relations. The point, as one of our respondents so aptly put it, is that although a firm may not have trade unions present it still has to manage the employment relationship. How employees are managed without unions and the nature of relations with employees where unions are absent is an area ripe for further study.

Note

1 Indeed, several commentators have noted that, in the future, employer support for union recognition is unlikely to be offered voluntarily, whether in high-technology firms or elsewhere. As a result, attention has been given to how statutory supports could be provided to enable unions first to build membership and then to pursue a recognition claim based on a step-by-step extension of bargaining rights (see, for example, TUC, 1991).

APPENDIX:
RESEARCH METHODS

The postal and follow-up interview surveys

The initial postal survey involved mailing 500 establishments in the South East of England in early 1989. A total of 115 usable responses were obtained, giving an effective response rate of 23 per cent. Since the objective was to survey larger firms rather than independent small businesses, only establishments which were part of firms with over 100 employees were mailed. The questionnaires included items on the composition of employment, union density and recognition, and technical and related organizational change. They were addressed to the personnel manager or person responsible for personnel matters at the establishment. In total the establishments that responded had 30,553 employees, and the firms of which they were a part a total of 150,438 employees. Compared to the high-technology sector as a whole (Butchart, 1987) our surveyed establishments accounted for 2.5 per cent, and the firms of which they were a part 12.1 per cent, of all high-technology employees in the UK. Further details can be found in McLoughlin and Gourlay (1990).

The follow-up interviews were undertaken in 1990 and 1991 at 30 establishments which were broadly representative of the 115 postal survey establishments (in order to boost the sample size two establishments were drawn from the pilot of the main postal survey). In most instances the personnel manager or person responsible for personnel matters was interviewed. In some cases it was possible to talk to both personnel and works management. The objectives of the follow-up interviews were to establish more precisely the extent of non-unionism at the establishment and, where appropriate, the parent company; to identify the types of personnel policy and practice present; and to explore the nature of management style, in particular the extent to which it might be defined in terms of an HRM type. To aid this, a further short questionnaire on personnel policies was completed at or near the time of the follow-up interview. This information was used to 'score' management approaches on our strategic integration and individualism/collectivism dimensions. The initial classification was made according to the presence or absence of particular policies or practices taken to be indicative of strategic integration and individual or collective regulation of a particular aspect of the employment relationship (see Table A.1). This classification was subsequently corroborated and adjusted with reference to data derived from our semi-structured interviews at the establishment and through reference to company documents, such as mission statements, employee handbooks and the like.

The case studies and employee surveys

The original intention had been to select the case-study companies from among the participants in the follow-up interview survey. In the event, only two of these organizations – CECO and COCO – agreed to participate in any further work and it was decided to include a third organization from outside the original postal sample. This decision was prompted by discussions with a local company which eventually became our DECO case study.

The three case studies involved interviews with management respondents from managing director to first line supervisor level conducted together with the observation of work and key technical operations over a period of several months during 1990 and 1991. In addition, employee surveys were undertaken at the

Table A.1   Individualism/collectivism and strategic integration
dimensions

Individualism/collectivism
Initial position on dimension determined by presence/absence of the
following:
- Profit-sharing for all categories of employee (manual, white-collar
  and professional)
- Share-ownership schemes for all employees
- Job-evaluation schemes for manual and/or white-collar employees
- PBR schemes for manual employees
- Quality circles
- Briefing groups
- Joint consultative committee
- 'Market-leader' pay policy
- Single-status terms and conditions
- Annual pay review for all employees
- Individual pay reviews
- Performance-related pay
- Appraisal used to determine pay
- Recognized unions

Strategic integration
Initial position on dimension determined by presence/absence of the
following:
- Formal procedure for discipline and dismissal
- Formal grievance procedure
- Formal pay policy
- Formal health and safety policy
- Formal communications/consultation policy
- Personnel specialist on site
- Personnel specialist with professional qualifications
- Personnel director on company board
- Nature and extent of personnel specialist involvement in technical
  change
- Written employment philosophy or 'mission' statement given to
  employees
- Training policy

---

three case-study enterprises by means of a questionnaire containing approximately 35 questions covering about 65 items. The questions asked for information on: employee background; job satisfaction; attitudes to pay determination; commitment to the company; and experience of and attitude towards trade union membership. Samples were drawn from employee lists provided by each company.

The employee survey at DECO focused upon the largest element of the core workforce, namely full-time design and draughting technicians who normally worked as part of project teams. Forty-four usable responses were received, giving an effective response rate of 51 per cent (one reason for the lower response rate was probably the fact that DECO employees were highly mobile and normally worked away from their base office). In the case of CECO separate surveys were conducted of the manual and non-manual workforces. Seventy-one usable responses were received from the manual employees, giving an effective response rate of 87 per cent; and 37 usable responses were received from the non-manuals, giving an effective response rate of 71 per cent. Finally, a total of 65 usable responses were received from the COCO computer staff, giving an effective response rate of 57 per cent. Further details of the statistical method used in the logit analysis can be found in McLoughlin and Gourlay (1991–2; 1993).

BIBLIOGRAPHY

ACAS (1989) *Annual Report of the Advisory, Conciliation and Arbitration Service*. London: ACAS.

Bacon, N. and Storey, J. (1993) Individualisation of the employment relationship and the implications for trade unions, *Employee Relations*, 15 (1), 5–17.

Bain, G. and Price, R. (1983) Union growth: dimensions, determinants and density, in G. Bain (ed.) *Industrial Relations in Britain*. Oxford: Blackwell, 3–33.

Barbash, J. (1984) Discussion, in T.A. Kochan, R.B. McKersie and H.C. Katz, US Industrial Relations in Transition, *Proceedings of Industrial Relations Research Association*, Winter, 294.

Barnett, C. (1986) *Audit of War*. London: Macmillan.

Bassett, P. (1986) *Strike Free: New Industrial Relations in Britain*. London: Macmillan.

Bassett, P. (1988) Non-unionism's growing ranks, *Personnel Management*, March, 44–7.

Bassett, P. and Cave, A. (1993) *All for One: The Future of the Unions*. Fabian Society Pamphlet no. 559. London: Fabian Society.

Batstone, E. (1988) *The Reform of Workplace Industrial Relations*. Oxford: Clarendon Press.

Batstone, E. (1989) The frontier of control, in D. Gallie (ed.) *Employment in Britain*. Oxford: Blackwell, 218–47.

Batstone, E. and Gourlay, S. (1986) *Unions, Unemployment and Innovation*. Oxford: Blackwell.

Bibliography

Beaumont, P.B. (1986) Industrial relations policies in high-tech firms, *New Technology, Work and Employment*, 1(2), 152–9.

Beaumont, P.B. (1987) *The Decline of Trade Union Organisation*. Aldershot: Gower.

Beaumont, P.B. (1990) *Change in Industrial Relations: The Organisation and Environment*. London: Routledge.

Beaumont, P.B. and Harris, R.I.D. (1988) High technology industries and non-union establishments in Britain, *Relations Industrielles*, 43(4), 829–46.

Beaumont, P.B. and Harris, R.I.D. (1990) Union recruitment and organising attempts in Britain in the 1980s, *Industrial Relations Journal*, 21(4), 274–86.

Beaumont, P.B. and Townley, B. (1985) Non-union American plants in Britain, *Relationes Industrielles*, 40(4), 810–24.

Bird, D., Beatson, M. and Butcher, S. (1993) Membership of trade unions, *Employment Gazette*, 101(5), 174–89.

Blyton, P. and Turnbull, P. (1993) HRM: Debates, Dilemmas and Contradictions, in P. Blyton and P. Turnbull (eds) *Reassessing Human Resource Management*. London: Sage, 1–15.

Brewster, C. and Larsen, H.H. (1992) Human Resource Management in Europe, *International Journal of Human Resource Management*, 3(3), 409–34.

Brown, W. (1988) *The Structure and Process of Pay Determination in the Private Sector: 1976–1986*. London: CBI.

Brown, W. (1993) The contraction of collective bargaining in Britain, *British Journal of Industrial Relations*, 3(2), 189–200.

Brown, W. and Walsh, J. (1991) Pay determination in Britain in the 1980s: The anatomy of decentralisation, *Oxford Review of Economic Policy*, 7(1), 44–59.

Buchanan, D.A. (1989) Principles and practice in work design: current trends; future prospects, in K. Sisson (ed.) *Personnel Management in Britain*. Oxford: Blackwell, 78–100.

Buckley, P.J. and Enderwick, P. (1985) *The Industrial Relations Practices of Foreign-owned Firms in Britain*. London: Macmillan.

Burns, T. and Stalker, G.M. (1961) *The Management of Innovation*. London: Tavistock.

Business Week (1981) The New Industrial Relations (special report), 11 May, 58–69.

Butchart, R.L. (1987) A new UK definition of the high technology industries, *Economic Trends*, no. 400, February, 82–8.

Causer, G. and Jones, C. (1992) Responding to 'skill shortages': recruitment and retention in a high technology labour market, *Human Resource Management Journal*, 3(3), 1–20.

Clark, J. (1993) Personnel management, human resource management and technical change, in J. Clark (ed.) *Human Resource Management and Technical Change*. London: Sage, 1–19.

Claydon, T. (1989) Union derecognition in Britain in the 1980s, *British Journal of Industrial Relations*, 27(2), 214–24.

Coopey, J. and Hartley, J. (1993) Reconsidering the case for organisational commitment, *Human Resource Management Journal*, 2(4), 18–32.

Cressey, P. (1985) Recasting collectivism: industrial relations in two non-union plants, in G. Spyropoulos (ed.) *Trade Unions Today and Tomorrow*, Vol. II. Maastricht: Presses Interuniversitaires Européennes, 63–83.

Cressey, P., Eldridge, J. and MacInnes, J. (1985) *Just Managing: Authority and Democracy in Industry*. Milton Keynes: Open University Press.

Crouch, C. (1989) United Kingdom: The Rejection of Compromise, in G. Baglioni and C. Crouch (eds) *European Industrial Relations*. London: Sage, 326–55.

Curran, J. (1991) Employment and employment relations in the small enterprise, in J. Stanworth and C. Gray (eds) *Bolton 20 Years On: The Small Firm in the 1990s*. London: Paul Chapman, 190–208.

Daniel, W. (1987) *Workplace Industrial Relations and Technical Change*. London: Frances Pinter.

Daniel, W.W. and Millward, N. (1983) *Workplace Industrial Relations in Britain*. London: Heinemann.

Daniel, W. W. and Millward, N. (1993) Personnel management and technical change: the findings from the WIRS series, in J. Clark (ed.), *Human Resource Management and Technical Change*. London: Sage, 43–77.

Department of Employment (1981) *Trade Union Immunities*. London: HMSO.

Department of Employment (1991) *Industrial Relations in the 1990s*. London: HMSO.

Department of Employment (1992) *People, Jobs and Opportunities*. London: HMSO.

Department of Trade and Industry (1990) *Britain: The Preferred Location*. London: Central Office of Information.

Dibden, J. and Millward, N. (1991) Trade union membership: developments and prospects, *Policy Studies*, 12(4), 4–19.

Dickens, L. and Bain, G. (1986) A duty to bargain? Union recognition and information disclosure, in R. Lewis (ed.) *Labour Law in Britain*. Oxford: Blackwell, 80–108.

Dickson, T., McLachan, H.V., Prior, P. and Swales, K. (1988) Big blue and the unions: IBM, individualism and trade union strategies, *Work, Employment and Society*, 2(4), 506–20.

Bibliography

Dillon, A. and Flood, P. (1992) Organisational commitment: do human resource practices make a difference? *Irish Business and Administrative Research*, 13, 48–60.

Disney, R. (1990) Explanations of the decline of trade union density in Britain: an appraisal, *British Journal of Industrial Relations*, 28(2), 165–77.

Dunn, S. (1989) Labour law legislation in the 1980s. Mimeo, London School of Economics, Department of Industrial Relations.

Dunn, S. (1990) Root metaphor in the old and new industrial relations, *British Journal of Industrial Relations*, 28(1), 1–31.

Dunn, S. (1991) Root metaphor in industrial relations: a reply to Keenoy, *British Journal of Industrial Relations*, 29(2), 329-36.

Dunn, S. (1993) From Donovan to . . . wherever, *British Journal of Industrial Relations*, 31(2), 169–87.

Edwards, P.K. and Marginson, P. (1988) Trade unions, pay bargaining and industrial action, in P. Marginson, P.K. Edwards, R. Martin, K. Sisson and J. Purcell (eds) *Beyond the Workplace*. Oxford: Blackwell, 123–64.

Edwards, R. and Podgursky, M. (1986) The unravelling accord: American unions in crisis, in R. Edwards, P. Garonna and F. Todtling (eds) *Unions in Crisis: Perspectives from Six Countries*. Dover, Mass.: Auburn House, 14–60.

Etzioni, A. (1961) *A Comparative Analysis of Complex Organisations*. New York: Free Press.

Evans, S. (1985) Use of injunctions in industrial disputes, *British Journal of Industrial Relations*, 23(1), 133–7.

Evans, S. (1987) The use of injunctions in industrial disputes, May 1984–April 1987, *British Journal of Industrial Relations*, 25(3), 419–35.

Evans, S. (1990) Employment regulation: Transformation or transition? Paper presented to 'Employment Relations in the Enterprise Culture' Conference, University of Wales, College of Cardiff, 18–19 September.

Findlay, P. (1992) Electronics: A 'culture' of participation?, in M. Beirne and H. Ramsay (eds) *Information Technology and Workplace Democracy*. London: Routledge, 56–91.

Findlay, P. (1993) Union recognition and non-unionism: Shifting fortunes in the electronics industry in Scotland, *Industrial Relations Journal*, 24(1), 28–43.

Foulkes, F. (1980) *Personnel Policies in Large Non-union Companies*. New York: Prentice Hall.

Fox, A. (1966) *Industrial Sociology and Industrial Relations*. Royal Commission Research Paper No. 3. London: HMSO.

Freeman, R. (1988) On the divergence of unionism amongst developed countries. Mimeo, Harvard University, October.

Freeman, R. and Medoff, R. (1984) *What Do Unions Do?* New York: Basic Books.

Freeman, R. and Pelletier, J. (1990) The impact of industrial relations legislation on British union density, *British Journal of Industrial Relations*, 28(2), 141–64.

Gallie, D. (1989) Trade union allegiance and decline in British urban labour markets. ESRC Social Change and Economic Life Initiative Working Paper 9. Oxford: Nuffield College.

Garrahan, P. and Stewart, P. (1991–2) Work organisation in transition: The human resource management implications of the Nissan way, *Human Resource Management Journal*, 2(2), 46–62.

Gilbert, R. (1993) Workplace industrial relations 25 years after Donovan: an employer view, *British Journal of Industrial Relations*, 31(2), 235–54.

Goss, D. (1991a) *Small Business and Society*. London: Routledge.

Goss, D. (1991b) In search of small firm industrial relations, in R. Burrows (ed.) *Deciphering the Enterprise Culture*. London: Routledge, 152–75.

Green, F. (1990) Trade union availability and trade union membership in Britain, *Manchester School of Economic and Social Studies*, 58, 378–94.

Green, F. (1992) Recent trends in British trade union density, *British Journal of Industrial Relations*, 30(3), 445–58.

Gregg, P. and Yates, A. (1991) Changes in wage-setting arrangements and trade union presence in the 1980s, *British Journal of Industrial Relations*, 29(3), 361–76.

Grenier, G.J. (1988) *Inhuman Relations: Quality Circles and Anti-unionism in American Industry*. Philadelphia: Temple University Press.

Guest, D. (1987) Human resource management and industrial relations, *Journal of Management Studies*, 24(5), 503–21.

Guest, D. (1989) Human resource management: Its implications for industrial relations and trade unions, in J. Storey (ed.) *New Perspectives on Human Resource Management*. London: Routledge, 41–55.

Guest, D. (1992) Employee commitment and control, in J.F. Hartley and G.M. Stephenson (eds) *Employment Relations*. Oxford: Blackwell, 111–35.

Guest, D. and Dewe, P. (1991) Company or trade union: which wins workers' allegiance? A study of commitment in the UK electronics industry, *British Journal of Industrial Relations*, 29(1), 75–96.

Hanson, C.G. (1991) *Taming the Trade Unions: A Guide to the Thatcher Government's Employment Reforms 1980–90*. London: Macmillan/Adam Smith Institute.

Hartley, J.F. (1992) Joining a trade union, in J.F. Hartley and G.M. Stephenson (eds) *Employment Relations*. Oxford: Blackwell, 163–83.

Hoerr, J. (1991) What should unions do? *Harvard Business Review*, May–June, 30–45.

Ingram, P. and Lindop, E. (1990) Can unions and productivity ever be compatible? *Personnel Management*, July, 32–5.

Incomes Data Services (1989) *Company Councils*, IDS Study 437. London: Incomes Data Services.

Incomes Data Services (1992) *Management and the Law*, IDS Quarterly 62, March. London: Incomes Data Services.

Jackson, M.P., Leopold, J.W. and Tuck, K. (1991–2) Decentralisation of collective bargaining: The case of the retail food industry, *Human Resource Management Journal*, 2(2), 29–45.

Keenoy, T. (1990) HRM: A case of the wolf in sheep's clothing? *Personnel Review*, 19(2), 3–9.

Keenoy, T. (1991) The roots of metaphor in the old and the new industrial relations, *British Journal of Industrial Relations*, 29(2), 313–27.

Kelly, J. (1988) *Trade Unions and Socialist Politics*. London: Verso.

Kelly, J. (1990) British trade unionism 1979–80: Change, continuity and contradictions, *Work, Employment and Society*, Special Issue, May, 29–65.

Kelly, J. and Bailey, R. (1989) British trade union membership, density and decline in the 1980s: A research note, *Industrial Relations Journal*, 20(1), 54–61.

Kelly, J. and Heery, E. (1989) Full-time officers and trade union recruitment, *British Journal of Industrial Relations*, 27(2), 196–213.

Kessler, S. and Bayliss, F. (1992) *Contemporary British Industrial Relations*. London: Macmillan.

Kleingartner, A. and Anderson, C.S. (eds) (1987) *Human Resource Management in High Technology Firms*. Lexington, Mass.: D.C. Heath.

Kochan, T.A. (1980) *Collective Bargaining and Industrial Relations*. Homewood, Ill.: Richard D. Irwin.

Kochan, T.A. and Chalykoff, J.B. (1987) Human resource management and business life cycles: some preliminary propositions. In A. Kleingartner and C.S. Anderson (eds) *Human Resource Management in High Technology Firms*. Lexington, Mass.: D.C. Heath, 183–200.

Kochan, T.A. and Tamir, B. (1989) Collective bargaining and new technology: Some preliminary propositions, in G.J. Bamber and R.D. Lansbury (eds) *New Technology: International Perspectives on Human Resources and Industrial Relations*. London: Unwin Hyman, 60–75.

Kochan, T.A., Katz, H.C. and McKersie, R.B. (1986) *The Transformation of American Industrial Relations*. New York: Basic Books.

Labour Research (1988) Union derecognition: New wave union busting, *Labour Research*, April, 13–15.

Lanning, H. and Norton-Taylor, R. (1991) *A Conflict of Loyalties: GCHQ 1984–1991*. Cheltenham: New Clarion Press.

Latrielle, P. (1992) Unions and the inter-establishment adoption of new micro-electronic technologies in the British private manufacturing sector, *Oxford Bulletin of Economics and Statistics*, 54(1), 31–51.

Legge, K. (1989) Human resource management: a critical analysis, in J. Storey (ed.) *New Perspectives on Human Resource Management*. London: Routledge, 19–40.

Legge, K. (1993) The role of personnel specialists: Centrality or marginalization?, in J. Clark (ed.) *Human Resource Management and Technical Change*. London: Sage, 20–42.

Lincoln, J.R. and Kalleberg, A.L. (1990) *Culture, Control and Commitment: A Study of Work Organisation and Work Attitudes in the United States and Japan*. Cambridge: Cambridge University Press.

Lloyd, J. (1987) Can the unions survive? *Personnel Management*, September, 38–41.

MacInnes, J. (1988) *Thatcherism at Work*. Milton Keynes: Open University Press.

MacInnes, J. (1990) The future of this great movement of ours, in P. Fosh and E. Heery (eds) *Trade Unions and Their Members*. London: Macmillan, 206–32.

Marchington, M. (1990) Analysing the links between product markets and the management of employee relations, *Journal of Management Studies*, 27(2), 111–32.

Marchington, M. and Parker, P. (1990) *Changing Patterns of Employee Relations*. Hemel Hempstead: Harvester Wheatsheaf.

Marginson, P. (1991) Change and continuity in the employment structure of large companies, in A. Pollert (ed.) *Farewell to Flexibility*. Oxford: Blackwell, 32–45.

Martin, R., Fosh, P., Morris, H., Smith, P. and Undy, R. (1991) The decollectivisation of trade unions? Ballots and collective bargaining in the 1980s, *Industrial Relations Journal*, 22(2), 197–208.

Mason, B, and Bain, P. (1991) Trade union recruitment strategies: Facing the 1990s, *Industrial Relations Journal*, 22(1), 36–45.

McIlroy, J. (1991) *The Permanent Revolution? Conservative Law and the Trade Unions*. Nottingham: Spokesman.

McLoughlin I. (1993) Technical change and human resource management in non-union firms, in J. Clark (ed.) *Human Resource Management and Technical Change*. London: Sage, 175–91.

McLoughlin, I. and Clark, J. (1994) *Technological Change at Work*, 2nd edition. Buckingham: Open University Press.

McLoughlin, I. and Gourlay, S. (1990) Innovation and change in

Bibliography

ROSELAND: a survey of high-tech establishments. Kingston Business School Occasional Paper No. 12.

McLoughlin, I. and Gourlay, S. (1991–2) Transformed employee relations? Employee attitudes in non-union firms, *Journal of Human Resource Management*, 1(2), 8–28.

Metcalfe, D. (1989) Water notes dry up: The impact of the Donovan reform proposals and Thatcherism at work on labour productivity in British manufacturing industry, *British Journal of Industrial Relations*, 27(1), 1–32.

Metcalfe, D. (1990) Can unions survive in the private sector?, in *Trade Unions and the Economy: Into the 1990s*, compiled by J. Philpott. London: Employment Institute, 9–18.

Metcalfe, D. (1991) British unions: Dissolution or resurgence? *Oxford Review of Economic Policy*, 7(1), 18–32.

Metcalfe, D. and Dunn, S. (1989) Calm wriggling, *New Statesman*, 28 July, 22–3.

Meyer, D.G. and Cooke, W.N. (1993) US labour relations in transition: Emerging strategies and company level performance, *British Journal of Industrial Relations*, 31(4), 531–52.

Millward, N. (1994) *The New Industrial Relations*. London: Policy Studies Institute.

Millward, N. and Stevens, M. (1986) *British Workplace Industrial Relations 1980–1984*. Aldershot: Gower.

Millward, N. and Stevens, M. (1988) Union density in the regions, *Employment Gazette*, 96(5), May, 286–95.

Millward, N., Stevens, M., Smart, D, and Hawes, W.R. (1992) *Workplace Industrial Relations in Transition: The DE/ESRC/PSI/ACAS Surveys*. Aldershot: Dartmouth Publishing.

Morgan, K. and Sayer, A. (1988) *Microcircuits of Capital: 'Sunrise' Industries and Economic Development*. Cambridge: Polity Press.

Mowday, R.T., Porter, L.W. and Steers, R.M. (1982) *Employee–Organisation Linkages: The Psychology of Commitment, Absenteeism and Turnover*. New York: Academic Press.

Newman, N. (1980) Britain's non-union leaders, *Management Today*, July, 59–112.

Nolan, P. and Marginson, P. (1990) Skating on thin ice? David Metcalfe on trade unions and productivity, *British Journal of Industrial Relations*, 28(2), 227–47.

Northcott, J. with Walling, A. (1988) *The Impact of Microelectronics: Diffusion, Benefits and Problems in British Industry*. London: Policy Studies Institute.

Peach, L.H. (1983) Employee relations in IBM, *Employee Relations*, 5(3), 17–20.

Pettigrew, A. and Whipp, R. (1991) *Managing Change for Competitive Success*. Oxford: Blackwell.

Phelps-Brown, H. (1990) The counter-revolution of our time, *Industrial Relations*, 29(1), 1–14.

Preece, D.A. (1993) Human resource specialists and technical change at greenfield sites, in J. Clark (ed.) *Human Resource Management and Technical Change*. London: Sage, 101–15.

Piore, M.J. and Sabel, C.F. (1984) *The Second Industrial Divide: Possibilities for Prosperity*. New York: Basic Books.

Purcell, J. (1987) Mapping management styles in employee relations, *Journal of Management Studies*, 23(2), 205–23.

Purcell, J. (1989) The impact of corporate strategy on human resource management, in J. Storey (ed.) *New Perspectives on Human Resource Management*. London: Routledge, 67–91.

Purcell, J. (1993) The end of institutional industrial relations, *Political Quarterly*, 64(1), 6–23.

Purcell, J. and Sisson, K. (1983) Strategies and practice in the management of industrial relations, in G.S. Bain (ed.) *Industrial Relations in Britain*. Oxford: Blackwell, 95–120.

Rico, L. (1987) The new industrial relations: British electricians' new style agreements, *Industrial and Labor Relations Review*, 41(1), 63–78.

Roberts, B.C. (1987) Mr Hammond's cherry tree: the morphology of union survival. London: Institute of Economic Affairs Occasional Paper 76.

Runciman, W.G. (1991) Explaining union density in twentieth century Britain, *Sociology*, 25(4), 697–712.

Schein, E.H. (1992) Coming to a new awareness of organisation culture, in G. Salaman (ed.) *Human Resource Strategies*. London: Sage, 237–54.

Sisson, K. (1989a) Personnel management in perspective, in K. Sisson (ed.) *Personnel Management in Britain*. Oxford: Blackwell, 3–21.

Sisson, K. (1989b) Personnel management in transition, in K. Sisson (ed.) *Personnel Management in Britain*. Oxford: Blackwell, 22–52.

Sisson, K. (1993) In search of HRM, *British Journal of Industrial Relations*, 31(2), 201–10.

Smith, P. and Morton, G. (1990) A change of heart: Union exclusion in the provincial newspaper sector, *Work, Employment and Society*, 4(1), 105–24.

Smith, P. and Morton, G. (1993) Union exclusion and the de-collectivisation of industrial relations in contemporary Britain, *British Journal of Industrial Relations*, 31(1), 97–114.

Smith, P. and Morton, G. (1994) Union exclusion: Next steps, *Industrial Relations Journal*, 25(1), 3–14.

Bibliography

Sproull, A. and MacInnes, J. (1987) Patterns of union recognition in Scottish electronics, *British Journal of Industrial Relations*, 25(3), 335–8.

Sproull, A. and MacInnes, J. (1989) Union recognition, single union agreements and employment change in Scottish electronics, *Industrial Relations Journal*, 20(1), 33–46.

Storey, J. (1989) Introduction: From personnel management to human resource management, in J. Storey (ed.) *New Perspectives on Human Resource Management*. London: Routledge, 1–18.

Storey, J. (1992) *Developments in the Management of Human Resources*. Oxford: Blackwell.

Storey, J. and Sisson, K. (1993) *Managing Human Resources and Industrial Relations*. Buckingham: Open University Press.

TUC (1988) *Meeting the Challenge*. First Report of the Special Review Body. London: Trades Union Congress.

TUC (1989) *Organising for the 1990s*. Second Report of the Special Review Body. London: Trades Union Congress.

TUC (1991) *Trade Union Recognition*. London: Trades Union Congress.

Waddington, J. (1992) Trade union membership in Britain 1980–1987: Unemployment and restructuring, *British Journal of Industrial Relations*, 30(2), 287–324.

Wickens, P. (1987) *The Road to Nissan: Flexibility, Quality, Teamwork*. London: Macmillan.

Willman, P. (1989) The logic of 'market-share' trade unionism: Is membership decline inevitable? *Industrial Relations Journal*, 20(4), 260–70.

Willman, P., Morris, T. and Aston, B. (1993) *Union Business: Trade Union Organisation and Financial Reform in the Thatcher Years*. Cambridge: Cambridge University Press.

INDEX

productivity
  difference between union and
    non-union settings, 17–18
Podgursky, M., 7
Porter, L.W., 110, 111
Price, R., 11
Prior, P., 93
Purcell, J., 24–5, 26, 30, 34, 57,
  160

Rico, L., 10
Roberts, B.C., 2
Runciman, W.G., 11

Sayer, A., 4
Schein, E.H., 92n
single union agreements, see
  collective agreements
Sisson, K., 24, 30, 33, 34, 57, 154
Smart, D., 12–13, 14, 15–16, 38,
  63, 143, 155, 160
Smith, P., 2, 10, 11, 13, 15, 160
Sproull, A., 41, 42
Steers, R.M., 110, 111
Stevens, M., 2, 4, 12–13, 14,
  15–16, 38, 63, 143, 155, 160
Storey, J., 27, 28–30, 31, 33, 35,
  122, 142, 146
strategic integration
  and 'benevolent autocracy', 54
  definition of, 28
  as a dimension of management
    style, 34, 36, 45, 59, 91, 146–7
  and 'opportunitists', 56
  and 'strategic HRM', 59
  and 'traditional HRM', 49–50
  see also human resource
    management
Swales, K., 93

Tamir, B., 7

technical change
  in non-union firms, 151–3
  in union and non-union
    settings, 18–19
  in the high technology sector,
    120–1
  see also CECO, COCO, DECO
    and human resource
    management
Townley, B., 37
Thatcher, Margaret, 1
trade unions
  impact of legal reforms on,
    10–11
  implications of non-unionism
    for, 155–8
  membership, decline of, 11–13
  membership density, decline
    of, 11–13
  recognition of, 13–14, 42–4
  see also collectivism, derecog-
    nition
TUC, 11, 17, 157, 163n
Tuck, K., 16
Turnbull, P., 27

Undy, R., 10
USA
  decline of trade unions in, 6–8
  implications for union decline
    in Britain, 8–9
  -owned firms in Britain, 37
  non-union firms in, 36

Waddington, J., 11, 12, 17
Walling, A., 121
Walsh, J., 15
Whipp, R., 30
Wickens, P., 17
Willman, P., 93, 157

Yates, A., 13, 15